KT-380-142

EAST SUSSEX COUNTY COUNCIL
WITHDRAWN
17 JUL 2024
19

04284038

My Busy Kitchen

Alex HOLLYWOOD

My Busy Kitchen

A lifetime of family recipes

For Mumma

CONTENTS

INTRODUCTION

I am a cook, not a chef. I am passionate about food and firmly believe that cooking and eating should be about one thing: enjoyment, not worrying about presentation and whether your roux is made to Michelin star standards. Nothing gives me greater pleasure than preparing a meal for family and friends, and then sitting back and watching everyone dig in. We all live busy lives, and those moments together are special, to be treasured, so why make life more complicated than it already is? Keep it simple – enjoy!

My recipes tend to fall into two categories – either quick and simple, like my easy salads or speedy week-night suppers, or slow and simple for lazy weekend lunches – stews and roasts that are perfect to leave simmering while you go for a long walk or sit around the table putting the world to rights. I cook the way my mother and grandmother taught me, with a hearty disregard for following

recipes to the letter. My grandmother, Mama Vanda, was an actress and a hugely flamboyant cook. She was an avid fan of Fanny Craddock and Robert Carrier, and would present us with platters of richly aromatic Persian lamb, dishes of Mont Blanc – sweetened chestnut purée with brandy and meringue – and brandy butter mountains to go with the Christmas pudding, which had been turned bright green with food colouring and decorated with pistachios, all the while dressed in a bejewelled silk kaftan in peacock blue.

Mama Vanda's mother, my great grandmother, was Norwegian, and trips to see the family in Norway always resulted in a whole freshly caught salmon being lugged back to Kent to be devoured with dill mayonnaise. Mama Vanda's Scandinavian heritage influenced other flavours that appeared in her food that I still love today – fresh and clean tastes to contrast with richer, headier aromas I have picked up from my own travels. My sister and I loved popping into her kitchen to see what we could 'forage', and there was always something delicious on the go for us to sneak a nibble of, such as homemade marzipan – much tastier than the bought stuff – rolled into balls and dipped in dark chocolate.

My father spent a lot of his youth in Madrid, which began his lifelong love of Spanish cooking. His paella was fabulous, and he made it in a massive

My Grandmother Vanda on the set of Le Fin Du Monde, *one of the first disaster movies! Shortly after, the Germans invaded France and she escaped back to England on the last train from Paris. She was and still is my hero! An amazing woman with a huge appetite for life.*

Daddy Andrew (my grandmother's Scottish father) salmon fishing in Aurland, Norway, with his hip flask of whisky to hand!

pan that I remember being brought home from southern Spain one summer, crammed in between me and my sister on the back seat of the car. We'd often eat it – chorizo, chicken, rabbit, fish, some smoky paprika and paella rice just thrown together and left to cook themselves – instead of a Sunday roast, and all the neighbours would pile around to join us in the garden. Although he is long gone, my father's passion for tapas remains with me, now mixed with my own mezze influences from the years Paul and I spent in Cyprus. I love to serve lots of little plates of delicious finger food – grilled meats, salads, dips and breads, all on colourful mismatched crockery – for everyone to help themselves and enjoy the contrasting flavours.

Monique was my French godmother, and the way I cook today owes a lot to her. From a very young age I would spend almost every holiday with her family in France, sometimes in Normandy or Champagne, but most often in the south. The first time I went, aged four, my mother packed me off with a huge leg of Kentish lamb nearly as big as me as a thank-you present – I doubt I could do the same with my son today! Monique introduced me to good bourgeois French cooking – rich intense flavours, cheeses that my father described as smelling of 'old socks' but that tasted utterly delicious, wine watered down for me and sweetened, so I learnt that it complemented the meals we ate, and bread, crisp and hot, collected every morning from the bakery on the corner.

All these influences are rich in the memories and cultures that I have experienced around the world, travelling through Europe and Africa with friends, working in Cyprus or as a chalet girl in the French Alps, or on family holidays in France or Spain, and they have had a huge impact on the ingredients and techniques I use in my own kitchen. I have learnt that you don't need to follow rigid rules: trust your instincts and you will probably be right – and a quick taste will reveal if you're not! Experiment and learn what flavours you like so that you can adapt and adjust the dishes you cook, making use of what you have to hand and what you feel like eating. No fresh basil? Use coriander instead. Add a little cinnamon and you change the flavour of the dish from Mediterranean to Middle Eastern. Use oats and nuts instead of breadcrumbs. And as for shortcuts, a carton of custard and a can of apricots have got me out of many a last-minute pudding situation. A few basic principles will go a long way in your kitchen, so my recipes will show you how a bit of this and a little splash of that will work together to produce effortlessly easy meals. You can, of course, follow my recipes to the very last detail, but I want you to know that you don't have to. If you're lacking an ingredient, you can use something else – and I'll give you some pointers in that direction so you know the kinds of things that can be swapped in or out and what goes well with what. Enjoy how flexible ingredients really are.

The secret is to be adaptable – my Twitter friends often ask me for inspiration about what to make for dinner that night, and I always reply, 'Go and check what's in your fridge.' Use what you have; it's pointless having a fridge full of ingredients if you're not going to use them. It's the way my mother and grandmother cooked, starting a meal with what they had in their cupboards, and many of their recipes are ones I still cook today.

The kitchen has been central to every generation on both sides of my family, and eating meals around the table has always been a way of bonding us together. Like most people, I think food forms an integral part of any celebration, but I believe we should try to make every meal into a bit of an occasion, not just on special days. You definitely

don't have to spend a fortune or have matching crockery, candles and crystal on the table, but you do need food that invites you to dig in, share it around, then sit back and enjoy. Along the way I've learnt a few short cuts that help me to get the food out more quickly, which means I can devote more time to the important things in life, such as spending as much time as possible with my friends and family, and those tips are what I will share with you in this book.

Good food is all about flavour, and a few simple twists can make the ordinary extraordinary. It really is all about spending time together, sitting and enjoying a meal with loved ones, not getting hot and bothered about an overcomplicated recipe that keeps you stuck in a steamy kitchen with a meat thermometer while friends and family await the outcome in another room. These are my recipes: quick, undemanding, easy and very adaptable to our busy lives. I want you to cook, sit, eat and enjoy!

TIPS TO GET YOU STARTED

Shopping

My mother and grandmother taught me to shop carefully and plan ahead, so I keep a well-stocked fridge, freezer and store cupboard, which means I can prepare a stress-free meal any night of the week. I will always grab a cut-price chicken or some fish and stick it in the freezer. The same goes for those herbs that have seen better days and are reduced to pennies. Buy them, chop and bag 'em up, then pop them in your freezer – but make sure you label them well as they can all look frustratingly alike when frozen.

Think about your ingredients in terms of what dishes they could make. For example, a bag of mixed vegetables could be the base for a soup, a fantastic tagine or a mixed couscous (see pages 72, 148 and 207). Or it could be the makings of a Pot au Feu with that reduced chicken you picked up earlier (see page 165). Buy ingredients that you know you will use, but do try things you might not have eaten before – game, such as venison and quail, or those tiny poussins, are always on the reduced aisle – grab them whenever you can and freeze them so you can try something different; food should be about having fun and trying new things.

Cooking and eating should both be a pleasure, so make sure you enjoy the shopping for them too.

Leftovers

Even in my house, where we do our utmost to avoid waste, we usually have some leftovers, so I make sure I choose my meals carefully and plan ahead so that I can use up whatever I have lurking in the fridge. For example, if we have a roast chicken on Sunday, I save the leftover meat from the carcass, re-roast the bones and make stock (see page 18) and I then have the beginnings of my Asti, asparagus and chicken risotto (see page 103), or the filling for a quick chicken pie into which you can throw the leftover veg too. Alternatively, the veggies can be chopped and used to fill some tart cases made with ready-rolled puff pastry – add a splash of cream and a little seasoning and bake for 15 minutes. Spanish Omelettes (see page 69) are a brilliant way to use up odd and ends, and make regular appearances at our dinner table. Just mix

whatever you have into the beaten eggs, along with some cooked potatoes, then fry until it's all lovely and crisp around the edges and eat with a green salad or French Beans with Thyme (see page 192). My grandmother even used to keep the cheese rind and add it with a splash of milk to her bolognese sauce – the result was rich and creamy, with a real depth of flavour. I find that most of my meals usually have more than one incarnation, and sometimes three or four! My approach is about being flexible and making the ingredients work hard for you.

Three golden rules: taste, taste, taste

A friend of mine, who is terrified of cooking, once told me that she follows recipes to the letter, but refuses to taste the food until sitting down to eat. Unsurprisingly, as she readily admits, the results are a bit hit and miss. When I left home and began cooking for myself and friends, I would be straight on the phone to my mother, asking advice on everything from how to make her French dressing to how long my casserole would take to cook. 'When it's done, darling,' was the standard answer, or, 'Taste a little and see.' She was right, of course. You must taste, adjust the seasoning, or even add or take away some of the ingredients. And don't be afraid to experiment: use my recipes as a guide, and play around with them to make them your own. If you don't want Pepper-blackened Salmon (see page 77), try cod or chicken breast. Similarly, swap the lamb in my tagine (see page 148) for chicken or quail. Play around with the flavourings too, using parsley or rosemary instead of tarragon in the Mustard Rabbit (see page 145), or leek and brandy instead of fennel and ouzo in my gratin on page 101 – or miss out the spirits and add a splash of white wine.

It's your kitchen and you're cooking for you and your loved ones, so experiment and make it taste the way you want.

HOW TO PLAY WITH FLAVOURS

Flavours are like colours: you can mix and match them, play around with them, and just by changing one for another can alter the entire 'mood' of a dish. For example, chicken cooked in tomato, basil and garlic has a distinctly Mediterranean flavour, but substitute coriander and saffron or turmeric and you have the makings of a Middle Eastern tagine.

Get to know your herbs and spices, and experiment at pairing them with different ingredients. If you always taste your dishes as you cook them, you will soon have the confidence to put a meal together without having to follow a recipe to the letter. Cooking is all about creating dishes with ingredients that you love to eat. There are no real rules to it, just familarise yourself with your

ingredients and you will 'own' your kitchen.

Below are some of my favourite combinations of herbs and spices, grouped by their approximate geographical origins. Try them in your cooking to create the type of flavour you want to achieve. Smell them and imagine what they will bring to your food. The descriptions I have given will help you to balance the dish — not too sweet, not too bitter, and not too hot.

Know your herbs and spices

You may be familiar with many of the herbs and spices in my list below, but I hope it will help you to experiment with flavours with more confidence — have some fun!

FRENCH

BOUQUET GARNI – a traditional blend of French herbs

HERBS DE PROVENCE – a southern warm and sunny flavour

OREGANO – dry and slightly aromatic

SAGE – a dry strong flavour

TARRAGON – tart and almost aniseed flavour

THYME – sweet and pungent

ENGLISH

BAY LEAVES – dry and aromatic

CHIVES – an oniony tang

PARSLEY – astringent and dry

PEPPERCORNS – hot!

ROSEMARY – an intense aromatic flavour

SAGE – a dry strong flavour

ITALIAN

BASIL – slightly spicy aromatic

MARJORAM – sweet basil

NUTMEG – woody and sweet, good in sweet and savoury

OREGANO – dry and slightly aromatic

ROSEMARY – woody and perfumed

THYME – sweet and pungent

NORTHERN EUROPE

CHIVES – an oniony tang

DILL – sharp and slightly lemony

PAPRIKA – peppery sweet or smokey

PARSLEY – astringent and dry

SPANISH

CORIANDER – slightly bitter aromatic

OREGANO – dry and slightly aromatic

PAPRIKA – peppery sweet or smokey

PARSLEY – astringent and dry

ROSEMARY – woody and perfumed

SAFFRON – rich colour and exotic, slightly bitter flavour

ASIAN COOKERY

CORIANDER – slightly bitter aromatic

GINGER – warm

KAFFIR LIME LEAVES – citrusy

LEMON GRASS – bitter citrusy

STAR ANISE – aniseed

INDIAN COOKERY

CARDAMOM – warm and astringent

CLOVES – aniseed and aromatic

CUMIN – earthy and woody

CURRY LEAVES – spicy and warm

DRIED CHILLIES – hot!

GARAM MASALA – a traditional Eastern blend

TURMERIC – bitter flavour

MIDDLE EASTERN

CINNAMON – sweet and spicy

CLOVES – aniseed and aromatic

CORIANDER – slightly bitter aromatic

CUMIN – earthy and woody

MINT – fresh and dry

RAS AL HANOUT – a traditional Middle Eastern blend

SAFFRON – rich colour and exotic, slightly bitter flavour

TURMERIC – bitter flavour

LARDER LOVES AND MUST-HAVES

I pick up jars and cans of interesting ingredients whenever I see them, but I make sure I'm never without the basics so I can put together a meal using only what I have in my cupboard. Here's a list of my essentials, plus a few ideas for how to turn them into simple meals.

Cans and jars

BEANS, CHICKPEAS, LENTILS, PEAS AND SWEETCORN — these are all great for making dhals and hummus, adding to salads, or stuffing into my Twice-baked Potatoes (see page 68). Use the beans (baked, borlotti or cannellini) in my Cowboy Beans on Toast (see page 31).

COCONUT MILK — great for cooking my Rice and Peas (see page 203).

CUSTARD — perfect for a trifle with sponge fingers, or mix with leftover bits of Meringue Roulade (see page 219) and freeze to make ice cream.

DUCK CONFIT — canned duck legs preserved in their own fat; with some sweet chilli sauce, cranberry sauce, a little red wine and a few berries, you can knock up my super-quick and very delicious duck supper (see page 105).

FRUIT — canned apricots, cherries, mangoes, peaches, pears and pineapple are great standbys. They can all be blitzed with sweetened cream and served as a mousse, added to a 'thrown-together' trifle, or sprinkled with sugar and baked until golden. Alternatively, arrange the drained fruit on a circle of ready-to-use puff pastry and bake for 20 minutes, or pop them in a dish with a sweetened batter and bake like a clafoutis (these last two ideas are lovely served with crème fraîche).

HONEY — can be used instead of sugar to sweeten anything, or serve with plain yoghurt and grilled fruit for pudding.

HOTDOG SAUSAGES — slice up and pan-fry frankfurters with eggs and paprika for breakfast. Also use them in my Beach Salad (see page 58).

JALAPEÑO PEPPERS — use in tortillas, or blitz with avocado, lime, Tabasco and salt and freshly ground black pepper to make guacamole.

MAYONNAISE — mix with canned tuna or cooked chicken for toasties, or combine with chopped eggs, coriander leaves and grapes for a salad.

MINCEMEAT — for a fab winter pudding, core out an apple and stuff with a chocolate truffle and some mincemeat. Top with brown sugar and butter and bake in the oven for 40 minutes — unbelievably good!

MUSTARD — I use mustard all the time in dressings, and to flavour all kinds of dishes. Keep French and English mustards in your store cupboard, making sure you have dried as well as ready-made English.

SALMON AND TUNA — really great for making quick fishcakes. Add to leftover Crushed Baby Potatoes (see page 199), season and mix in some chilli sauce or chopped herbs, chives or capers and an egg. Shape into patties, coat in breadcrumbs (see the freezer section, page 17), brush with butter and bake for 20 minutes in a hot oven. Lovely with lemony mayonnaise.

SUN-DRIED TOMATOES — use in salads and for my New Potato Salad (see page 48).

TOMATOES — with some olives, anchovies and chilli flakes you have the basics for pasta puttanesca. For a heartier dish, throw in some fish or shellfish to make seafood pasta.

Packets

CHOCOLATE – milk, dark and white chocolate can be added to any pudding to improve it, or simply melted to make a quick sauce. I also find it useful to keep a box of After Eights in the cupboard. Apart from meaning that you will always have some choccies to hand if you are invited out to supper by a lovely friend, you can also make a quick and light choccy mousse. Just melt the whole mints in a bain-marie, then add butter, fold in whipped cream and egg white and chill.

DRIED FRUITS – apricots, prunes and raisins, for example, are great for adding to granola, and can also be used in tagines and puddings.

DRIED GRAINS – couscous, pasta, pulses and rice offer endless combinations for suppers and salads.

OATS – great for making flapjacks (microwave butter, brown sugar and syrup, then add oats and cinnamon and press down, microwave again for couple minutes then cool and cut). Also good for adding to crumble mixtures and coating fishcakes.

SUGAR – caster and brown sugars are useful for baking, and to add sweetness to mealtimes.

Bottles

OIL – olive oil and neutral-flavoured rapeseed oil are store-cupboard essentials, but sesame and walnut oils are also useful, and don't forget chilli-, herb- and garlic-infused oils. They can all be used for cooking, making dressings and drizzling over food.

SWEET CHILLI SAUCE – mix with mayo to make a dressing for grilled fish, or add a dash to your own sauces for extra spice.

SWEET GINGER SAUCE – great with leftover chicken or turkey; simply brush the meat with the sauce and a little sesame oil, then grill until sticky and caramelised.

VINEGAR – balsamic, cider, malt, raspberry, sherry and wine vinegars will jazz up salads and give meat dishes a 'zing'. Try flavouring chicken thighs with a splash of balsamic, a little honey, cinnamon and seasoning, then fry in a pan. Really delicious!

WORCESTERSHIRE SAUCE – I use this in loads of dishes, such as my Cottage Pie and in the stuffing for Twice-baked Potatoes (see pages 172 and 68).

FREEZE IT ALL

We joke with my mother that if you stand around long enough in her kitchen, you'll end up in the freezer because she freezes practically everything, and I must admit that I do the same myself now.

If you don't have time to turn that chicken carcass into stock, bag it up and freeze it for another day. The same goes for chopped herbs, breadcrumbs and cheese – put them in bags to use whenever you need them – they are great in my Twice-baked Potatoes (see page 68), or in stews and saucy dishes that need a 'tweak'. Tomato Sauce (see page 21) can be used to cover pork escalopes, then topped with mozzarella and baked – lush! Frozen fish fillets are brilliant for a quick fish pie or to make into goujons (see pages 92 or 78). Portions of soup and lasagne can also be frozen for those times when you have unexpected mouths to feed. And stock (see pages 18–19) can be used in risottos, soups and stews.

It's amazing what you can throw together with bits and pieces: you just need to have the know-how, and I hope my book will give you that, along with a big helping of confidence, so you'll be able to magic up a meal in no time and have fun doing it.

BASIC STOCKS

When recipes are very simple, the quality of what you put in them makes a real difference. You can, at a push, get away with ready-made stock or even a cube, but making your own requires very little effort and tastes so much better. That chicken carcass, for example, could be bubbling away while you eat your main meal based on the rest of the bird. Freeze the stock in small containers so that you can use just as much as you need.

Chicken stock

This is the stock I use most often in soups, risottos and stews. It's easy to make, and makes world of difference to the flavour of your cooking.

Makes 1–2 litres

1 chicken carcass, with skin

1 carrot

1 onion, quartered

1 celery stalk

1 dried bay leaf

a few sprigs of fresh herbs, such as parsley and thyme

salt and freshly ground black pepper

Put all the ingredients in a flameproof casserole dish or heavy-based pan and add just enough water to cover them. Bring to the boil, then pop the lid on and simmer for 2–4 hours. Strain into a bowl, discarding the solids. Freeze the stock in small pots or plastic containers, adding a label and date.

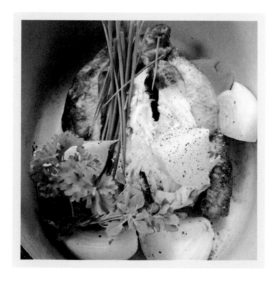

Vegetable stock

I often buy vegetables that are reduced in price or damaged and about to be thrown away because I hate to see waste, and they're ideal for stock. My advice is to use whatever you can get hold of – it's all good for something. This stock has a lighter taste than chicken stock, so use it in vegetarian dishes or when you have more subtle flavours going on.

Makes 1–2 litres
2 onions, quartered
2 carrots, roughly chopped
2 celery stalks
1 leek, chopped
400g mixed root veg
4 mushrooms
handful of parsley
1 tsp black peppercorns

Put all the ingredients in a flameproof casserole dish or heavy-based pan and add just enough water to cover them. Bring to the boil, then pop the lid on and simmer for about 1 hour. Strain, discarding the solids, then use as the basis of a hearty soup, or freeze the stock in small pots or plastic containers, adding a label and date.

Fish stock

Ask your fishmonger for fish trimmings to make this stock – he'll probably give you them for nothing – or save up prawn shells and fish bones in the freezer until you have enough.

Makes 1–2 litres
knob of butter
1 shallot, chopped
1 leek, chopped
½ fennel bulb, chopped
250g fish trimmings (heads, shells, etc.)
1 dried bay leaf
1 tsp black peppercorns
handful of fresh parsley
1 sprig of thyme
100ml white wine

Heat a flameproof casserole dish or heavy-based pan, add the butter and, when melted, gently fry the vegetables for a couple of minutes until just turning translucent. Add the fish trimmings, the bay leaf, peppercorns and herbs, stir together, then pour in the wine. Add enough water to cover all the ingredients and bring to the boil. Skim off any scum that forms on the surface, then lower the heat and simmer for about 30 minutes. Strain, discarding the solids, then freeze the stock in small pots or plastic containers, adding a label and date.

BASIC SAUCES

Here are simple recipes for the four sauces that form the basis of most of the meals I make. You can flavour them with whatever you like to suit the rest of the dish you are making – see page 13 for some ideas.

White sauce

Very easy to make, a white sauce is also the perfect base for adding flavours – cheese, nutmeg, mustard or brandy are some of my favourites. It's a great way of dressing up dull dishes.

Serves 4–6
50g slightly salted butter
50g plain flour
550ml milk
salt and freshly ground black pepper

Melt the butter in a small, heavy-based saucepan. Remove from the heat and gradually stir in the flour until you have a smooth paste. Slowly pour in the milk, whisking out any lumps that might form. Return to the heat, still whisking, and allow to simmer and thicken. Keep stirring over the heat for about 5 minutes to cook out the flour, then season and taste.

Variation: To make a richer sauce, you can use 100ml cream instead of milk, and add a splash of brandy or whisky.

Butter sauce

Perfect with fish and very simple to make, you can add garlic, capers or dill to give it some new flavours.

Serves 2–4
1 small onion, chopped
1 tbsp white wine vinegar
2 tbsp white wine
150g unsalted butter, cubed
squeeze of lemon (optional)
salt and freshly ground black pepper

Place the onion, vinegar and wine in a saucepan and heat quickly until slightly caramelised and reduced but not dried out. Add a splash of water, then stir in the butter, piece by piece, heating the mixture up slowly. Whisk until it becomes smooth and creamy. Season to taste and add a little lemon juice, if desired.

Serve with grilled fish topped with toasted almonds, or with grilled king prawns and freshly ground black pepper.

Tomato passata

To my mind, this is the most important sauce you need to know how to make because a good passata can make or break a meal. This one, made with ripe or even bruised tomatoes, is good enough to eat on its own with some pasta or grilled vegetables. You can use canned tomatoes if you like, but remember they will be quite acidic, so taste and adjust the sugar as necessary. Freeze what you don't need immediately so that you'll always have a quick meal to hand.

Makes about 1.5 litres
1kg ripe tomatoes
1–2 tsp sugar
1 tbsp balsamic vinegar
1–2 garlic cloves, unpeeled
2–3 tbsp olive oil
2 bay leaves
handful of basil leaves, crushed
salt and freshly ground black pepper

Preheat the oven to 180°C/Gas mark 4. Cut the tomatoes in half and arrange them in a single layer, cut-side up, in a large roasting tray. Sprinkle with the sugar and vinegar, throw in the garlic cloves, then drizzle with the olive oil. Season the lot and roast for 30–40 minutes, until the tomatoes start to caramelise.

Scrape the tomatoes into a heavy-based saucepan. Squeeze the garlic from its skin and add to the pan along with the bay leaves, basil and just enough water to cover the tomatoes completely. Bring to the boil, then simmer very gently for 1–1$^{1/2}$ hours, topping up occasionally with a little water if necessary. The longer you can leave the mixture to simmer, the better.

When done to your liking, blitz to a smooth sauce. Taste and adjust the seasoning or sweetness as necessary.

Homemade gravy

There is nothing like homemade gravy, flavoured with the roasted meat juices, a dash of wine and fresh stock. Freeze any that you have left over and serve it with toad in the hole or my Sausage and Onion Pie (see page 166).

Serves 4–6
1 tbsp flour or cornflour
400ml hot Chicken or Vegetable Stock (see page 18 or 19)
100ml red or white wine (depending on whether you're cooking red or white meat)
salt and freshly ground black pepper

Once your roast meat is cooked, transfer it to a warm serving plate, cover loosely with foil and set aside to rest. Skim off most of the fat in the roasting tray, then place the tray over the heat. When the liquid begins to bubble, add the flour and stir with the back of a spoon or a spatula to form a paste. Slowly add the stock, a little at a time, stirring and scraping up all the meaty, sticky bits that have stuck to the pan. Whisk to get rid of any lumps in your gravy, then splash in the wine and allow to bubble and reduce to the consistency you prefer. Season and pour into a warm gravy boat.

WAKEY-WAKEY

and BREAKFAST and BRUNCH

Blueberry blitz | Granola | Twice-baked almond croissants |
Cowboy beans on toast | Mini breakfast 'muffins'

They say breakfast is the most important meal of the day, and I couldn't agree more. Like my mother before me, I always make sure my son eats a wholesome, hearty breakfast to set him up for the day.

I have great childhood memories of breakfast time. In the winter my mother would make a big pot of creamy porridge for us, or eggs on toast. In summer we'd have chopped fresh fruit with yoghurt or Petit Suisse (a creamy white French cheese). And there would always be steaming bowls of hot chocolate and piles of toasted homemade bread with jam on the table.

For the weekends, Dad would make a special trip to the butcher in town who was renowned for his sausages. He would serve them with mounds of scrambled eggs sprinkled with paprika and we would wolf down the lot. With happy memories of all this, the idea of skipping breakfast fills me with horror. How can you get going on an empty stomach?

Even if you don't have a lot of time – and who does these days? – the super-quick Blueberry Blitz (see page 26) is packed with oats, fruit and yoghurt to give you the perfect kickstart, and a big batch of my Granola (see page 29) will take you only about half an hour to make but will last you all week. On a cold winter's morning, when there's a frost in the air, fiery Cowboy Beans on Toast (see page 31) will see you through to lunch and beyond. So throw those 'breakfast bars' in the bin. No more excuses – get up, get eating, get going!

BLUEBERRY BLITZ

My son Josh got hooked on milkshakes while on holiday in Cyprus, when he found it just too hot to eat his usual breakfast in the mornings. They have everything you need for a good start to the day. They're also great if you don't have time for a proper breakfast, as they're ready in seconds – and it's a brilliant way to use up anything in the fruit bowl that has seen better days.

Makes 2 large glasses

200ml milk

1 fruit yoghurt

1 banana

100g strawberries, hulled

50g blueberries

1 tbsp oats

50ml orange juice

sugar (optional)

Place all the ingredients in a blender and blitz together. Taste, and if the mixture isn't sweet enough, add ½ teaspoon sugar.

GRANOLA

I must admit that when I posted this recipe as a tweet, I didn't think it would be quite so popular, but everyone who has made it loves it. It's one of those recipes that you don't have to follow to the letter – you can 'wing it' and it's always delicious. Just use whatever fruits, nuts or seeds you have in your store cupboard, and if you want it a bit sweeter, just add a touch more syrup or honey. I like to serve it for breakfast with milk or honey and fresh chopped fruit, but it's also great as a snack when you have the munchies – much healthier than biscuits. This makes enough to last me for a week.

Makes 2 x 400g jars

325g porridge oats

100g mixed nuts (e.g. flaked almonds, hazelnuts, walnuts), crushed or chopped if large

250g mixed seeds (e.g. pumpkin, sesame, hemp)

100g dried fruit (e.g. raisins, cranberries, apricots)

3 tbsp sunflower oil

1 tsp vanilla extract

125ml maple syrup

75ml clear honey

pinch salt

Preheat the oven to 160°C/Gas mark 3.

Put all the ingredients, except the fruit, in a mixing bowl and stir well to combine. Tip on to a baking tray and bake for 10–15 minutes. Remove from the oven, mix in the fruit and bake for a further 10–12 minutes, watching that the granola doesn't overcolour (if necessary, give it a stir midway through the second half of cooking).

Set aside to cool, then store in clean screwtop jars or an airtight plastic container.

TWICED-BAKED ALMOND CROISSANTS

I love croissants, but unless they're eaten all in one sitting, I find they tend to go stale very quickly. This recipe is a great way of using up those hard ones and is based on an idea I picked up in France whilst staying with my godmother when I was little. Each morning I was sent down to the corner boulangerie to buy baguettes and ficelles (breadsticks) for lunch, and croissants to go with our bowls of hot breakfast chocolate. My favourite were the ones covered in sticky sweet almonds and filled with frangipane, so here they are.

Makes 4–6

4–6 stale croissants

60g flaked almonds, toasted (see tip below)

icing sugar, for dusting

For the frangipane

70g sugar

1 egg

½ tsp vanilla extract

70g butter

70g ground almonds

For the syrup

125ml water

30g caster sugar

Preheat the oven to 210ºC/Gas mark 7. Line a baking tray with baking parchment.

First make the frangipane. Beat the sugar and egg in a bowl until fluffy. Add the vanilla and butter, mixing until combined. Finally, stir in the ground almonds.

To make the syrup, heat the water and caster sugar in a pan over a gentle heat, stirring until completely dissolved. Transfer to a bowl.

Slice the croissants in half hoizontally and brush each half with the syrup. Place them on the prepared tray. Spread some of the frangipane mixture on the bottom half of each croissant, replace the top halves and spread a little more frangipane over the surface. Sprinkle with the flaked almonds.

Bake for 10–12 minutes, then dust with icing sugar and eat, dipping them in a big bowl of hot chocolate – heaven!

Tip: There are two ways of toasting seeds and nuts: the easiest is to dry-fry them in a hot pan, shaking and tossing them until fragrant or browned all over. The alternative way is to place them under a hot grill, shaking and turning them often, as they can quickly go from brown to burnt.

COWBOY BEANS ON TOAST

This is just the kind of breakfast you need after a big night. It will certainly wake you up and get you going! The dash of Tabasco and the chilli flakes give the beans a real kick, while the onion, cumin and paprika make them quite sweet and smoky. I also like to serve this as a Sunday evening snack or midweek supper.

Serves 2

½ small onion, chopped

olive oil, for frying

½ tsp crushed chilli flakes

½ tsp cumin seeds

1 x 415g can good-quality baked beans

dash of Tabasco

squirt of ketchup

smoked paprika

4 slices of brown bread

small handful of parsley, to garnish

crème fraîche (optional)

Put the onion and oil in a frying pan and fry until golden.

Meanwhile, using a pestle and mortar, crush the chilli flakes and cumin seeds to a powder. Add to the browned onion, along with the beans, Tabasco, ketchup and a pinch of the paprika.

Toast the bread while bringing the beans to bubbling point. Place the toast on plates, pour the beans over each serving and garnish with parsley, another pinch of paprika and a dollop of crème fraîche if you fancy.

MINI BREAKFAST 'MUFFINS'

These are so simple to make, and taste just as good eaten hot or cold. If you don't finish them all off for breakfast, take them to work or pack them up for a picnic lunch instead. You can bung in a load of chopped veg if you don't have sun-dried tomatoes – asparagus tips and chopped courgettes work particularly well here – and instead of the mozzarella you can use ricotta. The only thing you need to make sure of is that you use finely sliced ham, such as Parma or Serrano ham, to form the baskets as other types won't crisp up.

Makes 12

2–3 packets (about 18 slices) of Serrano or Parma ham
3 large eggs
150g double cream
150g crème fraîche
1 x 190g jar sunblush tomatoes
pinch of paprika
1 ball mozzarella cheese

Preheat the oven to 180°C/Gas mark 4.

Lightly grease a 12-hole muffin tray. Line each hole with 1–2 strips of ham, ensuring the bottom is covered, then lightly scrunch the ham around the sides to create a rim.

Put the eggs, cream, crème fraîche and paprika into a bowl and mix well (don't season – the ham is salty enough). Pour the liquid into the prepared tray, filling the holes nearly to the top.

Cut some of the tomatoes into strips and drop a few into each hole. Tear up the mozzarella and place a little on top.

Bake for 15–20 minutes, until risen and golden. Serve warm with buttered toast fingers and a cuppa.

SIMPLE SALADS

Green salad with garlic croutons and dijon dressing | Potato and asparagus spears with homemade pesto salad | Yellow melon salad with grilled halloumi, mint and capers | Radish, orange and coriander salad | Tricolore | Chickpea salad with white tuna and lime | New potato salad with sun-dried tomatoes and yoghurt dressing | Summer panzanella

I often feel disappointed when I order a salad. Sadness is a limp lettuce leaf, a few pieces of tasteless tomato and some chopped cucumber. But it doesn't have to be that way. Salads don't need to be relegated to a side dish or a token bit of green on your plate; they can be colourful, vibrant and with as many tastes and textures as you please so that every forkful is a surprise.

Greek salads filled with sweet red onions, sharp capers and creamy feta inspire me to experiment with different cheeses and flavours. Middle Eastern salads often combine meat, pulses and fruit all in one dish — they are a complete meal in themselves. And my all-time favourite green salad has loads of textures going on — green beans, spinach, cucumber — with extra crunch from croutons scattered on top (see page 38). Or try adding nuts for another layer of texture. Walnuts are slightly bitter and quite dry, so they are wonderful with sweet flavours, such as the fruit in my Grapefruit and Stilton Salad (see page 99). Pine nuts, on the other hand, are creamier, which makes them perfect alongside slightly acidic tomatoes and a balsamic dressing.

There are no hard and fast rules with salads, so experiment and throw in whatever you like. Once you have the main ingredients, spend a minute thinking about the dressing: will it clash or complement? My Panzanella with Parma ham, melon and figs (see page 51) cries out for something sweet, so I add a basil and honey dressing to bring out the flavour of the figs and enhance the salty ham. A green salad, though, often calls for something sharper, such as a mustard- or vinegar-based dressing to lift out the flavours.

When I lived in Cyprus, my dear friend Ligia, who is godmother to our son, taught me that the simplest way to make a dressing is to roll a lemon firmly on the work surface, cut it in half and squeeze the juice all over the salad. Follow with a generous glug of olive oil, a good grinding of salt and freshly ground black pepper and there you have it.

Add whatever flavours you like to your dressing, and don't be afraid to 'cheat' by including shop-bought items with your own ingredients. To liven up chopped little gem lettuce, for example, try mixing a little sweet chilli sauce into a lemon juice dressing, or add a spoonful of mayonnaise to some olive oil, crushed garlic, chopped chives and black pepper. Just make sure you taste as you go because dressings are all about balance — not too sweet and not too sharp.

All the salads and dressings in this chapter are simple and versatile, so feel free to experiment and create your own salad heaven. Don't make do!

GREEN SALAD WITH GARLIC CROUTONS *and* DIJON DRESSING

A classic green salad of a few mixed lettuce leaves can be a bit boring, so focus on getting a range of textures into your bowl. This dressing is one that I go to again and again – it works with almost any combination of salad ingredients or lightly cooked green veg.

Serves 4–6

150g runner beans, left whole

4–6 slices stale wholemeal bread (see page 233)

3 tbsp olive oil

½ tsp garlic salt

100g baby spinach leaves

1 romaine lettuce, chopped

4 spring onions, chopped

½ cucumber, deseeded and chopped

50g rocket leaves

salt and freshly ground black pepper

For the dressing

1 tbsp white wine vinegar

1 tsp Dijon mustard

½ tsp sugar

1 shallot, chopped

handful of basil leaves, chopped

4 tbsp olive oil

Preheat the oven to 190°C/Gas mark 5.

Steam, boil or even microwave the runner beans until tender. Rinse in cold water and set aside.

Chop the stale bread into chunks and place in a bowl. Sprinkle with the olive oil, garlic salt and a good grinding of pepper. Mix well, transfer to a baking tray and bake for about 10 minutes, until golden brown. Set aside.

To make the dressing, place all the ingredients except the oil in a blender and blitz until smooth. Add the olive oil and mix again to amalgamate, season to taste, then pour into a small jug.

Place all the remaining salad ingredients in a bowl, add the beans and mix well. Sprinkle the cooled croutons over the top, add a grinding of salt and freshly ground black pepper and serve with the vinaigrette.

POTATO *and* ASPARAGUS SPEARS WITH HOMEMADE PESTO SALAD

I love pesto – it's so versatile, and such an easy way to add flavour. Spread it over chicken or fish before cooking them in the oven, toss it through steamed green veg, or, of course, stir it through pasta for an instant supper. Fresh pesto is not at all difficult to make, and will keep for several weeks if stored in the fridge; just put it in a screwtop jar and keep it topped up with oil.

I think of this salad as a real 'throw-it-together' recipe. The ingredients listed below make a great basic combination, but you can add whatever else you like – anchovies, artichokes, roasted vegetables, strips of Parma ham – the possibilities are endless.

Serves 4–6

olive oil, for frying

125g asparagus tips

500g baby new potatoes, cooked and cooled

50g rocket leaves

1 x 190g jar sunblush tomatoes, drained

Parmesan cheese, freshly grated

For the pesto

100g pine nuts

200ml extra virgin olive oil

75g Parmesan cheese, grated

1 large bunch of basil leaves

squeeze of lemon juice

2 garlic cloves

salt and freshly ground black pepper

First make the pesto. Dry-fry the pine nuts until golden, then transfer to a blender or food processor. Add the remaining ingredients, apart from the seasoning, and blitz to a smooth purée. Season to taste, then place in a screwtop jar, top with a spoonful of oil to seal, and store in the fridge.

Heat a little oil in a griddle pan and chargrill the asparagus for a few minutes until tender and slightly blackened.

Put the remaining salad ingredients into a serving bowl, add the asparagus and 2 tablespoons pesto and mix well. Season, sprinkle with some Parmesan and serve immediately.

Variations: To make red pepper pesto, preheat the oven to 180°C/Gas mark 4 and roast 2 or 3 peppers with a splash of oil until blackened (about 15–20 minutes). Peel off the skin and use the flesh instead of the basil listed above. I also like to add a pinch of chilli and some fresh coriander leaves.

YELLOW MELON SALAD WITH GRILLED HALLOUMI, MINT *and* CAPERS

This salad reminds me of sunny days when I lived in Cyprus and, more recently, of holidays on the little island of Kefalonia, where they make the best mint and caper salad in the world. It's best served with some simply grilled fish or meat and eaten in the garden with a glass of wine ... happy days.

Serves 4–6

150g halloumi cheese, sliced

½ yellow melon, such as honeydew, deseeded and cut into chunks

50g pea shoots

50g baby salad leaves

handful of mint, chopped, plus a few extra leaves to garnish

1 small red onion, very finely sliced

1 tbsp capers, drained

For the dressing

4 tbsp olive oil

juice of 1 lemon

salt and freshly ground black pepper

First make the dressing. Put all the ingredients for it in a screwtop jar, shake well, then set aside.

Heat a griddle pan until hot. Add the halloumi slices and dry-fry for a few minutes on each side so that the cheese becomes golden and lacy around the edges. Set aside off the heat.

Place the remaining salad ingredients in a serving bowl. Shake the dressing, pour it over the salad and toss well.

Arrange the warm halloumi slices on top and garnish with the extra mint leaves. Add a little extra seasoning, then serve.

RADISH, ORANGE *and* CORIANDER SALAD

Here is the simplest of salads, but with such fresh and clean flavours that it gives a lift to everything it is served with. The combination of peppery radish, tangy orange and the slightly bitter coriander provides the perfect backdrop for lamb, chicken, pork … anything, really. Try it with grapefruit instead of orange, and with some walnuts scattered over at the end.

Serves 4–6

12 radishes, finely sliced

1 red onion, finely sliced

4 large oranges, segmented, deseeded and membrane removed

bunch of flat leaf parsley, leaves only, chopped

bunch of coriander, leaves only, chopped

For the dressing

50 ml fresh orange juice

splash of olive oil

salt and freshly ground black pepper

Put the radishes, onion, orange segments and herbs into a salad bowl and mix together.

Put all the dressing ingredients into a jam jar, seal tightly and shake well. Pour the dressing over the salad and mix well. Cover and chill in the fridge for 1 hour before serving.

TRICOLORE

One summer a few years ago we went to Italy, and almost every day for lunch I would chop up loads of fresh tomatoes and a huge ball of mozzarella to go with slices of Parma ham and bresaola. This salad – using red, white and green ingredients, the tricolore *of the title – is equally simple, perfect with some cured meats or simply cooked fish. Just make sure you choose a very good-quality mozzarella and perfectly ripe tomatoes.*

Serves 4–6

4–5 large ripe tomatoes, sliced

1 large ball of buffalo mozzarella, sliced

10 basil leaves, torn

For the dressing

2 tbsp extra virgin olive oil

1 tsp aged balsamic vinegar

sea salt and freshly ground black pepper

Arrange the tomato and mozzarella slices alternately on a plate, then sprinkle with the basil leaves.

Pour the oil and vinegar into a screwtop jar, season well and shake to emulsify. Pour over the salad, then toss and serve immediately.

Variation: For an alternative dressing, mix some of your homemade pesto with a little more olive oil.

CHICKPEA SALAD WITH WHITE TUNA *and* LIME

I think canned tuna is very underrated. I use the ordinary supermarket stuff for lots of standby meals – mixed with mayonnaise and paprika, for example, and sprinkled with chilli Cheddar, it makes a great topping for toasties. For this recipe, which has quite a Middle Eastern feel to it, you need to use good-quality canned white tuna.

Serves 4

1 x 420g can chickpeas, drained

1 x 180g can line-caught white tuna, drained

1 red onion, sliced

6–8 cherry tomatoes, quartered

handful of parsley, chopped

1 tbsp chopped chives

For the dressing

1 tbsp lime juice

2 tbsp extra virgin olive oil

salt and freshly ground black pepper

Place all the salad ingredients in a serving bowl and mix well.

Combine all the dressing ingredients in a screwtop jar, shake well, then taste and adjust the seasoning. Pour over the salad, toss again and serve.

Variations: To expand on the Middle Eastern flavour of the salad, you can add some chopped fresh coriander or toasted cumin seeds if you have any. You can also use spring onions if you don't have red onions.

NEW POTATO SALAD WITH SUN-DRIED TOMATOES *and* YOGHURT DRESSING

This salad came about by accident one afternoon when I didn't have enough ingredients for my usual potato salad. I threw together whatever I had to bulk it up and I now think this version is much tastier than the original. The yoghurt makes it light and refreshing, and the sun-dried tomatoes add an unexpected burst of flavour.

Serves 4–6

450g Jersey new potatoes

4 tbsp Greek yoghurt

4 tbsp mayonnaise

1 tsp lemon juice

1 hardboiled egg, finely grated

handful of flat leaf parsley, chopped

6–8 sun-dried tomatoes, finely sliced

salt and freshly ground black pepper

Cook the potatoes in a pan of boiling salted water until tender. Drain and cool, then cut in half and place in a bowl.

Mix the yoghurt, mayonnaise and lemon juice together in a bowl. Add the egg, parsley and tomatoes and mix well. Season, then stir into the potatoes and serve.

SUMMER PANZANELLA

Here is a great salad if you have lots of hungry mouths to feed but not much in the house because the bread bulks it out and makes it really filling. There are lots of different tastes and textures going on here, and you can add whatever flavours you like to make each mouthful a bit of surprise. For example, torn chicken breast instead of ham works really well with this dressing.

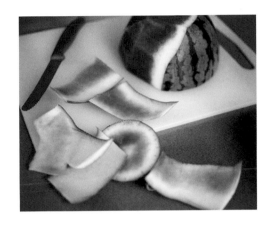

Serves 6–8

2–3 tbsp olive oil

1 stale ciabatta loaf, cubed

¼ watermelon, deseeded and chopped into chunks

1 cucumber, peeled and chopped

1 small red onion, finely sliced

150g pitted black olives

½ packet feta, diced

4 fresh figs, quartered

¼ small iceberg lettuce, chopped

small handful of chopped coriander

salt and freshly ground black pepper

For the dressing

1 tbsp honey

2 tbsp olive oil

1 tbsp lemon juice

handful of basil, chopped

salt and freshly ground black pepper

Preheat the oven to 220ºC/Gas mark 7.

First make the dressing. Put all the dressing ingredients for it in a blender, add seasoning and blitz until smooth. Taste and adjust as necessary, then transfer to a screwtop jar.

Pour the oil into a baking tray, add the bread and toss to coat. Season, then bake, turning from time to time, until toasted all over.

Put the remaining ingredients into a salad bowl. Add the crispy bread cubes, toss with the dressing and serve.

On the Beach

Pain farci | Sticky wings n' drumsticks | My basic beach salad recipe | Homemade lemonade | Best-ever brownies

I grew up by the sea, and even now, wherever I go, I subconsciously locate where the nearest beach is. My mother and grandmother were firm believers that fresh air was an absolute necessity for growing children, so, rain or shine, chunky woollen jumper or bathing suit, many an afternoon was spent digging sandcastles or crabbing on the rocks. I still love going to the beach, and most weekends my friends and I will round up all the kids and pack them into the car with loads of sweaters and wellies if it's chilly, and a picnic hamper of course.

All sorts of things go into the plastic boxes, including Sticky Wings 'n' Drumsticks (see page 57), which can be cooked and chilled the day before (if you don't want to use drumsticks you can use sausages instead); Pain Farci (see page 55), a loaf stuffed with leftovers, which is filling and full of good things; and my staple Beach Salad (see page 58), made with tomatoes, feta, sweet onions and whatever else takes my fancy, is also a regular (the ingredients can be whatever you feel like – roasted veg, baby spinach leaves, chopped meats, salamis, cream cheese – to create layers of texture and taste). To round it all off are my Best-ever Brownies (see page 61), cut into tiny bite-sized chunks and unbelievably moreish.

So whatever the weather, pack up your bags and hit the beach!

Top left: me aged two on Westgate beach with my mum Gloria Moores - the same beach I take Josh to now. We even buy ice lollies from the same place and we always take home made lemonade down with us, just like we used to.

Pain farci

Why have sandwiches when you can have this delicious stuffed loaf, really impressive for grown-ups and kids alike? I use leftover roast meat, salami, vegetables, cheese – it all goes in and it's always a hit. It looks great too as you slice into it, though I slice it and wrap it before putting it into the hamper so it's easy finger food.

Serves 6

1 smallish round or oval white loaf

1 large mozzarella ball, sliced

handful of basil or rocket leaves

1 large tomato, sliced

100g chargrilled or sun-dried tomatoes, drained

200g ricotta or cream cheese

slices of Parma ham, salami and/ or chicken breast

10 pitted black olives, halved

salt and freshly ground black pepper

Slice off the top of the loaf and hollow out the middle, leaving a little of the doughy bread inside.

Now start layering your ingredients inside the loaf: first the mozzarella, then the basil, tomato and so on until you reach the top. Season only the final layer (because the ham is already salty). If you have a slight gap at the top, don't worry – simply replace some of the bread you scooped out. Replace the 'lid' and wrap the loaf loosely in cling film.

Place the loaf between 2 chopping boards and weigh it down with books for a couple of hours. This will make it easier to slice.

Rewrap the compressed loaf tightly and place it in the fridge to chill. Cut into slices for a picnic, or reheat to crisp it up and eat with a green salad.

Sticky wings n' drumsticks

I tend to prepare these in large batches, eating some for dinner and saving the rest for lunch or the beach the next day. They're great hot or cold, especially with potato salad. Don't forget the napkins!

Serves 6–8

800g chicken drumsticks

450g chicken wings

250ml tomato ketchup

150ml maple syrup

1 tbsp dark soy sauce

juice of 1 small lime or lemon

1 tsp crushed garlic

2 tbsp sesame oil or olive oil

1 tsp finely chopped fresh ginger, or a splash of orange juice

salt and freshly ground black pepper

Preheat the oven to 190ºC/Gas mark 5.

Skin the drumsticks and place them in an ovenproof dish with the wings.

Put all the remaining ingredients into a bowl, season generously and mix well. Pour the mixture over the chicken pieces and mix thoroughly.

Roast for 35–40 minutes, basting a couple of times. Serve on a big platter with Twice-baked Potatoes (see page 68).

My basic beach salad recipe

Every time I have a beach day out, I make this salad. I love it, my friends love it, the kids love it, and we eat it straight out of the plastic box with a fork each.

Serves 6

300g penne pasta, cooked and chilled

200g feta or mozzarella cheese, crumbled or torn

50g rocket leaves

50g baby salad leaves

4–6 sausages, grilled, chilled and sliced, or a handful of chorizo slices

30g pine nuts (or walnuts)

1 red onion, thinly sliced

20 pitted black olives

½ small orange melon, cut into chunks

handful of mint leaves, chopped

For the dressing

2–3 tbsp olive oil

juice of 1 lemon

sea salt and freshly ground black pepper

First make the dressing. Put the oil, lemon juice and seasoning in a screwtop jar and shake well.

Mix all the salad ingredients in a bowl, transfer to a plastic container and keep cool until lunchtime. (Don't dress the salad until just before eating it or it will become soggy.)

Variation: I sometimes include chopped hulled strawberries instead of the olives.

Homemade lemonade

Have this on a hot day with lots of ice and you'll never want the bought stuff again.

Makes 1 litre
3–4 unwaxed lemons, depending on size
150g caster sugar
1 litre sparkling mineral water

Roll 2 of the lemons on a hard surface to release the juice inside. Squeeze out the juice and place it in a blender with the remaining whole lemon, the sugar and half the water. Blitz until the fruit is finely chopped.

Push this mixture through a fine sieve into a large jug. Add the rest of the mineral water, taste and adjust the sweetness if necessary. Serve with lemon slices and ice cubes, or put into a cooler for the beach.

Best-ever brownies

Makes about 24

100g unsalted butter, plus extra for greasing

150g dark chocolate (70% cocoa solids)

175g caster sugar

75g light muscovado sugar

1 tbsp golden syrup

2 large eggs

1 tsp vanilla extract

100g plain flour

2 tbsp cocoa powder

½ tsp baking powder

This is my sister's recipe, and it really is the best. She also makes a mean Cognac Truffle (see page 154).

Preheat the oven to 180°C/Gas mark 4. Butter a shallow 20cm x 28cm brownie tin and line it with greaseproof paper.

Put the butter, chocolate, both sugars and the syrup into a saucepan and heat gently until blended. Set aside to cool.

Put the eggs and vanilla into a bowl and beat together until frothy. Gently whisk in the cooled chocolate mixture.

Sift the flour, cocoa powder and baking powder into the chocolate mixture and fold together very gently until well combined.

Pour the batter into the prepared tin and bake for 20–25 minutes, until it looks browned and starts to come away from the sides of the tin. Allow to cool, then turn out and cut into small squares – trying your best not to eat the whole lot in one go!

QUICK MID-WEEK MEALS

Coconut dahl with mint and coriander relish | Twice-baked loaded potatoes | Monday leftovers Spanish omelette | Stuffed Portobello mushrooms with spinach and walnuts on sourdough | Smoky corn chowder | Carbonara with fresh egg yolk | Smoked salmon pasta with sage and goats' cheese | Pepper-blackened salmon | Cod goujons with mushy peas | Chicken in a basket | Kentish apple pork chops | Porky burgers | Mozzarella meatballs | Cypriot lamb koftas with tzatziki in pitta bread

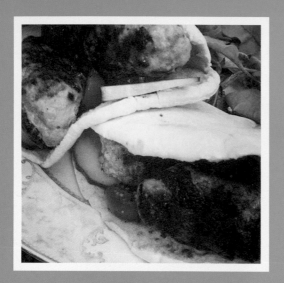

Our weeknight meals tend to be rather thrown-together affairs – often with me still in my coat, multi-tasking while I put the shopping away or help out with homework. Most people can relate to arriving home with just half an hour to throw a meal together, which is probably why my speedy suppers are the most popular of the recipes that I put on Twitter. Everything in this chapter is quick, fuss-free and tasty enough for my son to eat the whole lot without complaint, so I think they're winners. They are also endlessly flexible, so you can change the ingredients to use whatever you have, or adapt the recipe to make use of leftovers.

A big favourite in our house is Carbonara with Fresh Egg Yolk (see page 73) – it really does take just minutes to make – and using fresh pasta will make it even quicker. One Twitter friend posted that she'd tried it and for the first time had scraped-clean bowls from her family – a high accolade indeed! If I have extra children around after school, the easiest meal to make – and the one that all kids love – is Mozzarella Meatballs (see page 85), which can be padded out with a few more breadcrumbs if you don't have quite enough mince to go round. My breaded Chicken in a Basket (see page 79) is also a big hit, possibly because it's reminiscent of what you get in a certain fast food outlet, but far healthier and, I think, much tastier too.

We all get stuck in a rut sometimes and become fed up with cooking the same things week in week out, but if you have the basics in your larder, fridge and freezer, you can create food from all over the world in less than half an hour. Having said that, there's nothing wrong with the odd fish finger sarnie or a bought pizza every so often, but as you'll see from the recipes in this chapter, it doesn't take long to chuck together something really tasty and allow yourself time to sit down and enjoy it. *Bon appetit!*

COCONUT DAHL WITH MINT and CORIANDER RELISH

I think lentils and pulses are very under-appreciated and we should all eat more of them. They are great as side dishes and for bulking up soups and stews, and they respond really well to whatever flavours you put with them. This warming curry is creamy and spicy, but not too heavy – and it's perfect with a dollop of the zingy relish on top.

Serves 4

2 tbsp vegetable oil

1 tsp cumin seeds

1 tsp mustard seeds

1 red onion, finely chopped

1 garlic clove, finely chopped

250g dried red lentils, washed and drained

600g canned coconut milk

2 tomatoes, finely chopped

2 green chillies, deseeded and chopped

150ml water

1 tsp garam masala

1 tbsp natural yoghurt

salt and freshly ground black pepper

1 tsp coriander leaves, to garnish

2–4 limes, quartered

For the relish

25g coriander stems and leaves, chopped

10g mint leaves

1 garlic clove, crushed

1 tsp finely chopped fresh root ginger

1 green chilli, deseeded

1 tsp garam masala

1 tsp dried chilli flakes

juice of 1 lemon

Heat the oil in a heavy-based saucepan and fry the cumin and mustard seeds until they start to pop. Add the onion and garlic and fry for a further 2–3 minutes.

Add the lentils, coconut milk, tomatoes, chillies and measurement water, season and bring to the boil. Simmer uncovered for 30 minutes, stirring occasionally to ensure the lentils don't stick.

Meanwhile, make the relish. Put all the ingredients for it in a food processor or blender, add some seasoning and blitz to a smooth consistency. Transfer to a bowl and keep chilled.

About 5 minutes before the end of the cooking time, stir in the garam masala and yoghurt. Serve with a spoonful of the relish and garnish with the fresh chopped coriander leaves and lime quarters.

TWICE-BAKED LOADED POTATOES

One of my classic 'use-up-what-you-have-in-the-fridge' recipes. My son adores these and you really can add whatever you like to the stuffing – roasted veg, cooked meats, leftover cheese ... you name it! If you don't have lardons, use chopped bacon or sliced ham or chicken breast – it will all taste lovely. Before baking the potatoes in the oven, I often give them a five-minute head-start in the microwave (make sure you prod them several times with a fork so they don't explode), then I finish them off in the oven. Easy peasy!

Serves 4–6

4 medium baking potatoes

200g mixed vegetables (e.g. chopped spring onions, cooked leeks, cooked green beans, sweetcorn, peppers)

50g grated Cheddar cheese

50g mozzarella cheese, torn

1 tbsp cream cheese

2 slices ham, chopped, or some cooked crispy lardons

30g butter

1 tbsp chopped chives

salt and freshly ground black pepper

2 tbsp grated Parmesan cheese, for sprinkling

Preheat the oven to 180°C.

Prick the potatoes with a fork and, if cooking from scratch, pop then in the oven for 1 hour. If microwaving, pop in the microwave for 5–8 minutes on High, until the flesh slightly 'gives' when you squeeze it. Transfer to the oven for another 15–20 minutes, depending on size, to crisp up a bit.

Cut the potatoes in half and scrape the flesh out into a bowl. Return the skins to the oven on a baking tray.

Meanwhile, add all the remaining ingredients, except the Parmesan, to the potato flesh and mix until smooth. Season well.

Remove the skins from the oven, load each half with the potato mixture, then sprinkle with the Parmesan. Return to the oven for another 10–15 minutes, or until golden brown and crispy. Serve with a green salad or green beans.

MONDAY LEFTOVERS SPANISH OMELETTE

Here is where all the yummy Sunday roast leftovers come together into a delicious supper in minutes. Spanish omelettes were a forte of my dad's — he would throw everything into a huge pan and in a few minutes a delicious crisp, stuffed omelette was ready for turning on to a plate. I'd have it with lashings of 'Tommy K' (ketchup) and my favourite Garlic Courgettes (see page 195). The beauty of this recipe is that you can use up whatever oddments of food you have in the fridge, and — depending on how many you are feeding — add or reduce the eggs and veg.

Serves 4—6

5—6 large eggs

1 tbsp crème fraîche (optional)

1 tbsp olive oil

1 large onion, sliced

1 garlic clove, crushed

6—8 roast potatoes, roughly sliced

½ tsp sweet paprika

150g cooked green beans, peas, leeks, carrots, etc., chopped

2 slices of bacon, chorizo or ham, chopped

handful of parsley, chopped

salt and freshly ground black pepper

Crack the eggs into a bowl and add the crème fraîche (if using), salt and pepper.

Heat the oil in a large ovenproof frying pan (preferably non-stick) and sauté the onion and garlic until softened.

Add the potatoes and paprika and fry for about 1 minute, then add the remaining vegetables, the bacon and parsley. Pour in the egg mixture and stir well to ensure it covers the whole pan evenly. Put the lid on your pan (if it has one), then lower the heat and cook for 10 minutes or so. If it has no lid, cook the omelette for 5 minutes uncovered, then place under a hot grill for 3—4 minutes. The finished omelette should be brown and crisp underneath and almost set on top.

Before serving, run a spatula right around the omelette to ensure the edges are free. Turn it on to a warm plate and serve with crispy salad leaves in a basil honey dressing (see page 51).

Me aged 8 and my sister Liz aged 4 in Northern Spain, in the spring — another one of our meandering foodie expeditions!

STUFFED PORTOBELLO MUSHROOMS WITH SPINACH *and* WALNUTS ON SOURDOUGH

My parents were big mushroom-eaters, and my mother would often prepare them as a light main course, stuffed, as they are here, and served on day-old bread toasted and rubbed with garlic. Mushrooms are cheap, full of flavour and quick to cook, and they really do deserve to be centre stage once in a while rather than always being chopped up and slung into stews and chicken dishes.

Serves 4

8 large Portobello mushrooms

4 tbsp olive oil

8 slices of pancetta, chopped

500g chestnut mushrooms, chopped

3 garlic cloves, 2 crushed, 1 cut in half

4 slices of sourdough bread

1 large handful baby spinach leaves

5 tbsp crème fraîche

shavings of Parmesan cheese, to serve

50g walnuts, toasted (see page 30) and crushed

salt and freshly ground black pepper

Heat the grill to its highest temperature and cover the rack with foil.

Brush the Portobello mushrooms lightly with the oil, add seasoning, then grill for 6–8 minutes. Set aside.

Heat a frying pan until hot. Add the pancetta and fry until the fat runs. Add the chestnut mushrooms and crushed garlic and fry until both are soft but not brown.

Toast the bread under the grill, rub the garlic halves over both sides of the toast and arrange on a large serving dish. Place the Portobello mushrooms gill-side up on the toast.

Add the spinach and crème fraîche to the pancetta mixture, stir and season. Spoon some of the mixture into each mushroom, garnish with the Parmesan shavings and the walnuts and serve straight away.

SMOKY CORN CHOWDER

This is my standard chowder recipe, but if you don't have all the ingredients, that's fine. Add extra onion if you don't have leeks, replace the thyme with parsley and the canned sweetcorn with frozen, use whole milk instead of cream ... just do your own thing, but remember to taste as you go, adjusting the seasoning as necessary.

Serves 4–6

knob of butter

olive oil, for frying

100g smoked lardons

1 onion, sliced

1 leek, chopped

400ml full-fat milk

175ml double cream

1 bay leaf

½ tsp dried thyme

pinch of paprika

2 potatoes, diced

350g smoked haddock, flaked and boned

1 x 198 g can sweetcorn, drained

salt and freshly ground black pepper

1 tsp chopped chives, to garnish

Heat the butter with a dash of oil in a saucepan. When hot, fry the lardons until browned all over. Add the onion and leek and sauté until soft.

Add the milk, cream, bay leaf, thyme, paprika and potatoes to the pan and simmer until the potatoes have softened.

Discard the bay leaf, then add the fish and sweetcorn and simmer for a further 5–8 minutes.

Taste and adjust the seasoning, garnish with the chives and serve with warm crusty bread.

CARBONARA WITH FRESH EGG YOLK

This is Josh's all-time favourite supper and his number one request if he's been away. It's real comfort food and a great meal to have ready quickly after a footie match when he comes home absolutely starving. I make it the way they do in France, with a fresh egg yolk mixed into the sauce to give it an altogether richer, more satisfying yumminess.

Serves 2
olive oil, for frying
200g lardons
250ml double cream
4 fresh pasta nests
1 large egg yolk
30g Parmesan cheese, grated
salt and freshly ground black pepper
chopped parsley, to garnish

Heat a little oil in a frying pan, add the lardons and fry until crispy and brown. Drain off any excess fat, then pour in the cream and allow to bubble gently.

Cook the pasta in a pan of boiling salted water to which you've added a dash of olive oil. Boil for 2 minutes, then drain, reserving a cupful of the pasta water.

Take the cream sauce off the heat and allow to cool a little, then add the egg yolk, stirring quickly. If the sauce is too hot, the egg will start to scramble. If this happens, use some of the pasta water to bring it back.

Add the pasta to the pan and stir well to coat it with the creamy lardon sauce. Sprinkle in the Parmesan, season just a little and dish up with a sprinkling of fresh parsley and a little more black pepper.

SMOKED SALMON PASTA WITH SAGE *and* GOATS' CHEESE

Here's one of those meals that really can be assembled at the very last minute and served in little bowls with forks — no fuss and no bother. You can curl up in an armchair to eat this — just make sure you have a cold glass of wine and a good film to watch.

Serves 4

400g pasta shells

olive oil, for drizzling and frying

50g pine nuts

1 garlic clove, crushed

8 sage leaves, torn

200g smoked salmon, torn into strips

200g soft goats' cheese

salt and freshly ground black pepper

Cook the pasta shells in boiling salted water until al dente. When cooked, drain and drizzle with a splash of olive oil.

Heat a little oil in a pan and gently fry the pine nuts and garlic until browned. Take off the heat, throw in the sage leaves, pasta and salmon, and season well. Crumble in the goats' cheese, stir to combine and serve straight away.

Variation: Try using Boursin instead of the goats' cheese — it's really good.

PEPPER-BLACKENED SALMON

Although this looks impressive, it's such an easy dish to throw together. It makes a tasty family meal, and can even be dressed up for an impromptu supper party by serving with a beautiful green salad with crunchy croutons (see page 38). Added to that, it's low in calories … oh, and kids love it, so you'll get them eating fish without a fuss – a winner all round!

Serves 4–6

4–6 salmon fillets

2 tbsp olive oil

juice of ½ lemon

50g butter, melted

about 20 black peppercorns

½ tsp garlic powder

small handful of parsley, chopped

salt and freshly ground black pepper

Preheat the oven to 180°C/Gas mark 4.

Place the salmon fillets in a single layer in a baking dish.

Put all the remaining ingredients in a screwtop jar, seal tightly and shake vigorously. Pour the liquid over the salmon and allow to sit for 5 minutes.

Oil and heat an ovenproof griddle pan until very hot. Place the salmon in the pan, skin-side down, and cook until golden and crisp.

Transfer the pan to the oven and cook for a further 10 minutes, until the fish flakes and is cooked through. Serve with Horseradish Mash (see page 202) and asparagus spears.

Daddy Andrew (my great grandfather) with Great Great Grandfather Anders, fishing for salmon in Norway.

COD GOUJONS WITH MUSHY PEAS

Goujons are simple and quick to make, and these ones have a crunchy polenta coating instead of the traditional breadcrumbs. Fresh fish is delicious, but I always make sure I keep some frozen white fish fillets in my freezer as a standby: if I know I'm going to be in a rush, I'll take a couple out and defrost them in time for supper.

Serves 4

4 cod or other white fish fillets (about 150–200g each), cut into strips about 10 x 3cm

50g ground polenta

zest of 1 lemon

1 egg, beaten

2 tbsp olive oil

salt and freshly ground black pepper

4 lemons, quartered, to serve

For the mushy peas

400g frozen peas

knob of butter

½ tsp mint sauce

salt and freshly ground black pepper

Preheat the oven to 190ºC/Gas mark 5.

Put out 3 shallow bowls or plates. Combine the polenta, lemon zest and seasoning in one; put the beaten egg in another; and the oil in the third. Dip the strips of fish first into the egg and then into the polenta, making sure they are well coated. Brush with the olive oil and place on a baking tray. Bake for 12–15 minutes, until golden.

Meanwhile, cook the peas in a pan of boiling water for 5 minutes, until tender. Drain, transfer to a bowl and add the butter, mint and seasoning. Mash well.

Serve the goujons with the mushy peas, chips and lemon wedges.

CHICKEN IN A BASKET

There are always some chicken pieces in my freezer, and they form the basis of many a mid-week supper. This recipe is definitely one of the favourites in our house, especially if I have children over. Serve with spicy potato wedges and a mini salad for little fingers.

Serves 4–8

oil, for greasing

150g breadcrumbs

50g porridge oats (optional)

1 tsp dried oregano

1 x 200g jar Hellmann's mayonnaise

zest of ½ lemon (optional)

½ tsp garlic purée, or 1 garlic clove, crushed

1 tbsp Dijon mustard

1 tsp smoked paprika

8 chicken thighs, skinned

salt and freshly ground black pepper

Preheat the oven to 190°C/Gas mark 5. Lightly grease a baking tray.

Put the breadcrumbs and oats on a plate, add the oregano and seasoning, and mix well. Set aside.

Place the mayonnaise in a bowl, add the lemon zest, garlic, mustard and paprika and stir together.

Dip the chicken pieces first into the mayo mixture, ensuring they are well covered, then into the breadcrumbs. Place them on the prepared tray and bake for 30 minutes, until golden brown and crispy. Serve in a basket and devour with your fingers.

Variation: I sometimes add grated Cheddar to the breadcrumb mix to make the chicken bites cheesy and extra crunchy.

KENTISH APPLE PORK CHOPS

I love my home county of Kent, and make sure to use the local produce whenever I can, particularly the fruit: apples, plums and pears all end up in my saucepan. Freshly pressed apple juice really is delicious, and I use the dry variety for this recipe. If you can't get hold of it, cider or even white wine can be used instead, but make sure it's sharp and dry.

Serves 4–6

4–6 large pork chops

2 tbsp olive oil

1 large onion, sliced

3–4 sage leaves

150ml dry apple juice

2–4 Cox's apples, cored and sliced into circles

1 tbsp crème fraîche

salt and freshly ground black pepper

Preheat the oven to 180°C/Gas mark 4.

Season the chops. Heat half the olive oil in a flameproof casserole dish and fry the chops until nicely browned all over. Set aside on a plate.

Fry the onion in the empty dish for a few minutes until translucent. Add the sage leaves, return the chops to the dish and pour over the apple juice. Adjust the seasoning, cover and simmer for 18 minutes, until the pork is cooked through.

Meanwhile, heat the remaining oil in a frying pan. When hot, quick-fry the apple slices on both sides, until golden. Arrange the apples on a serving platter and keep warm.

Lift the chops out of the casserole and sit them on the apples. Quickly reduce the liquid left in the casserole to a sauce, then add the crème fraîche. Taste and season if necessary. Pour the sauce over the pork and serve with Parmesan crushed new potatoes.

PORKY BURGERS

I always make mini burgers because children love them, and they are perfect for little hands. But with the heady flavours of smoked paprika, coriander and garlic, they are just as popular with adults. This recipe is really a bit of a nod to the years I spent living in Cyprus, eating under the vines in Paphos. Souvla (grilled pork) is a very popular dish over there, rich and aromatic, and these burgers are more reminiscent of that than the traditional American-style burger.

Makes about 6–8

500g minced pork

30g good-quality brown breadcrumbs

1 large egg, beaten

8g coriander, chopped

2 garlic cloves, finely chopped

½ tsp smoked paprika

1 small red onion, finely chopped

zest of 1 lemon and juice of ½

3 tbsp olive oil

salt and freshly ground black pepper

To serve

2 tbsp mayonaise

1 tsp Dijon mustard

mini burger buns

slices of cucumber, tomato and cornichon

Preheat the grill to its highest setting. Oil the grill pan but do not put under the grill yet.

Place all the burger ingredients in a bowl and mix thoroughly using your hands. Shape into small burgers about the size of your buns, then place on the prepared pan and grill for 3–4 minutes on each side, until cooked through and charred outside.

Put the mayo and mustard in a small dish and mix together.

Open out the buns and place a burger on each bottom half. Add a dollop of the mustard mayo, a slice or two of cucumber, cornichon and tomato, then top with the other half of the buns. Tuck in straight away.

MOZZARELLA MEATBALLS

If you are really pushed for time, you can buy ready-made meatballs and jazz them up with this recipe. But if you are able to make them from scratch (they're very easy), they're even better and pretty darn good!

Serves 4–6

2 tbsp olive oil

300g minced pork

300g minced beef

100g brown breadcrumbs

30g Parmesan cheese, grated

1 large egg

1 tsp dried mixed herbs

1 tsp ready-minced garlic, or 1 garlic clove, crushed

1 tsp Worcestershire or soy sauce

handful of parsley, chopped

150g mozzarella cheese

flour, for dusting

salt and freshly ground black pepper

For the sauce

1 tbsp olive oil

200g tomato Passata (preferably homemade, if you have time – see page 21)

½ glass red wine

1 tsp pesto (optional)

½ tsp sugar

6 capers, chopped

Preheat the oven to 190°C/Gas mark 5. Put both lots of mince in a large bowl, add the breadcrumbs, Parmesan, egg, herbs, garlic, Worcestershire sauce and parsley and mix well, using your hands.

Pinch off a small handful of the meat mixture and roll between your hands into a ball about the size of a golfball. Flatten it into a pattie, then tear off a small piece of mozzarella and place it in the centre. Reshape into a ball, enclosing the cheese. Repeat this process with the remaining meat mixture and mozzarella. Dust the work surface with flour and roll the meatballs in it.

To make the sauce, heat the oil in a lidded ovenproof casserole dish. When hot, brown the meatballs all over. Add the remaining ingredients, season generously and stir well. Cover the dish and pop into the oven for 20–25 minutes. Serve with spinach tagliatelli or orzo and vegetables.

Variation: Chopped onion can be used instead of capers.

CYPRIOT LAMB KOFTAS WITH TZATZIKI IN PITTA BREAD

Koftas could be described as elongated meatballs or skinless sausages that are cooked on skewers. They are traditionally eaten as street food, stuffed into pittas with masses of salad and eaten on the go. In Cyprus there is no end of tiny restaurants and kebab shops selling snacks at any time of the day or night. In fact, the sweet aroma of lamb with cinnamon and lemon takes me straight back to those winding village streets, with tables and chairs set out in the road and people eating, drinking and enjoying life.

Serves 4

500g minced lamb

¼ tsp ground cinnamon

1 garlic clove, crushed

1 tbsp lemon juice

1 tsp cumin seeds, crushed

1 tbsp olive oil, plus extra for brushing

small handful of coriander, chopped

For the tzatziki

250g Greek yoghurt

½ cucumber, peeled, deseeded and finely chopped

3 garlic cloves, crushed

olive oil

salt and freshly ground black pepper

To serve

8 warmed pittas

slices of tomato, red onion and cucumber

First make the tzatziki. Combine all the ingredients for it in a bowl and mix well. Cover and chill until needed.

Put the lamb and all the remaining kofta ingredients into a large bowl, season generously and mix together using your hands then shape the mixture into 8 sausage shapes.

Brush the koftas with olive oil and griddle them in a hot pan for about 4 minutes on each side. Serve stuffed into the pitta breads with slices of tomato, onion and cucumber, and a good dollop of tzatziki on top.

Variation: Minced beef can be used instead of lamb.

'COME-AS-YOU-ARE' KITCHEN SUPPERS

Smoky fish pie with a dash of Scotch | My kitchen moules with pull-apart bread | Paprika pan-fried chicken with grapefruit, stilton and asparagus salad | Chicken, fennel and ouzo gratin | Normandy chicken | Asti, asparagus and chicken risotto | Roast quail and beetroot with a warm lentil salad | Confit de canard with red wine and berries | Rack of lamb with a Dijon and Parmesan crust | Auntie Alex's lasagne | Quick 'n' easy chilli with chocolate and a tequila shot | Beef curry with toasted cumin yoghurt

There is nothing I like more than having an impromptu crowd around for a relaxed kitchen supper – no fuss, no bother, no dressing up, no setting a table with silver and napkins. I adore the informality of it all, winter or summer – a few tea-lights in jam jars, an assortment of plates, everyone helping to get the table laid and bringing over bowls of salad, potatoes or enough bottles of red wine to sink a battleship.

For a smaller group on warm summer days, perhaps after a trip to the beach, My Kitchen Moules (see page 94) can be thrown into a pot and minutes later are ready to serve with plenty of crusty Pull-apart Bread (see page 94), followed by juicy peaches and raspberry ice cream. When the nights get cooler as autumn approaches, I often have curry evenings, and each guest contributes a small dish. I make my gorgeously fiery Beef Curry (see page 110) and lay it on the table with gargantuan amounts of Coconut Rice and Peas (see page 203), along with Paul's naan breads and all the extras for everyone to dig in. And for weekend guests arriving late in the evening, I'll prepare a huge dish of creamy, cheesy Lasagne (see page 108) to serve with a tomato and mozzarella salad. When I know their ETA, I'll pop the lasagne in the oven so that it's golden, bubbling and fragrant, ready to welcome the weary travellers after their journey.

But miserable January and February are my very favourite times to do low-key Friday-evening suppers. Christmas has come and gone, everyone is fed up with the rotten weather, and no one wants to drive very far from home. That's when my Smoky Fish Pie with a dash of Scotch (see page 92) is the answer to all your winter blues. It's real stick-to-your-ribs food – pungent, hearty and the Scotch warms you to your toes. Have a good bottle of whisky to hand and serve with a dram.

Entertaining is what you make of it, so if you don't feel like donning a pair or heels or tails, don't! Keep it simple and relaxed – as long as the food is tasty and filling and there's enough of it, you know everyone will enjoy the evening and come back for more.

SMOKY FISH PIE WITH A DASH OF SCOTCH

My great-grandfather, whom we called Daddy Andrew, was a Scotsman who adored salmon fishing. He married a girl from Norway, and since everyone in Norway loves to eat fish, particularly salmon, it was a match made in heaven. This dish is a nod to Daddy Andrew, who was also rather keen on his whisky, which he always kept in a flask at his side.

Serves 4–6

1kg potatoes, chopped

700ml milk, plus a little extra for mashing

1 onion, cut in half

1 bay leaf

200g smoked haddock fillets, cut into large chunks

400g mixture of salmon, cod, prawns and scallops

1 egg

200g smoked mackerel fillets, cut into large chunks

75g butter

40g plain flour

4 tbsp Scotch whisky

200ml double cream

25g Parmesan cheese, grated

1–2 tsp chopped chives

salt and freshly ground black pepper

Boil the potatoes in a saucepan of water until tender. Drain and set aside to cool.

Preheat the oven to 180°C/Gas mark 4.

Pour the milk into a large pan, add the onion and bay leaf, and bring to a simmer. Add the haddock, salmon and cod and poach for 5–8 minutes, until cooked through.

Meanwhile, soft-boil the egg in a separate pan of boiling water (the yolk should be runny but the white set). Cool under running cold water, then peel off the shell. Chop the egg on a plate and set aside.

Using a slotted spoon, remove the fish from the milk and place it in an ovenproof dish with the prawns, scallops and mackerel. Sprinkle the egg over the mixture.

Remove the onion and bay leaf from the milk, then add about 40g of the butter and sprinkle in the flour, whisking until it thickens into a sauce. Pour in the whisky, season and stir for another 2–3 minutes. Mix in the cream, then pour the sauce over the fish. Set aside to cool.

Add the remaining 35g butter and a splash of milk to the cooled potatoes and mash until smooth. Season and add the Parmesan and chives. Using a large spoon or spatula, spread the potato mixture over the fish and bake for 30–40 minutes, until bubbling and brown.

Serve with slices of brown bread and butter, a big green salad and an icy cold bottle of Chablis.

MY KITCHEN MOULES WITH PULL-APART BREAD

My mother firmly believed that children should eat the same food as adults, so I was introduced to mussels as a very young child on our family holidays to France and Spain. After an initial whinge, I loved them and haven't looked back since. Some people have the idea that cooking mussels is difficult, but it's really not – and this recipe proves it in the tastiest way possible. Serve in big bowls with lots of buttery pull-apart bread to mop up all the lovely juices.

Serves 4–6

75g butter

2 garlic cloves, crushed

2 onions, finely chopped

400ml dry white wine

1 bouquet garni

2kg fresh mussels, rinsed and scrubbed

squeeze of lemon juice

salt and freshly ground black pepper

handful of parsley leaves, chopped, to serve

For the pull-apart bread

1 baguette

75g butter

1 tsp mustard

2 tsp poppy seeds

2 garlic cloves, crushed

2 spring onions, finely chopped

1 tbsp chopped parsley

squeeze of lemon juice

handful of grated Gruyère cheese

First prepare the bread. Make deep criss-cross cuts along the baguette, then wrap it in foil, leaving the top of the parcel open. Melt the butter in a saucepan and whisk in all the other ingredients except the cheese. Pour this mixture into the cuts, then stuff them with the cheese. Put the open parcel in the oven and bake for 8–10 minutes.

Meanwhile, melt the butter in a large saucepan, add the garlic and onions and fry until translucent. Stir in the wine, add the bouquet garni and heat until bubbling. Season well, then add the mussels, cover with a lid and cook until the shells open – this shouldn't take any longer than a few minutes. Give the pan a good shake every so often to move them around, then use a slotted spoon to transfer them to a bowl, discarding any that haven't opened.

Boil the liquid left in the pan until reduced by about half. Add a little lemon juice, taste and season accordingly. Pour the liquid over the mussels, sprinkle with the parsley and serve immediately with the pull-apart bread.

Tip: Keep the hinged shell of the first mussel you eat to use as a pincer for eating the rest.

PAPRIKA PAN-FRIED CHICKEN WITH GRAPEFRUIT, STILTON *and* ASPARAGUS SALAD

This is one of those quick dishes that I threw together almost by accident one evening, and has since become a real favourite of mine. I adore paprika, I was going to use orange but only had a grapefruit, and I then rummaged in my fridge for the rest of the ingredients. It's really delicious and I've since tried it with peaches too. Yummy!

Serves 6

oil, for greasing

12 baby asparagus spears

6 chicken breasts

1 tsp smoked paprika

1 x 200g packet mixed salad leaves

1 pink grapefruit, segmented

8 spring onions, chopped

2 celery sticks, chopped

½ cucumber, peeled, deseeded and chopped into chunks

50g pine nuts, toasted (see page 30)

2½ tbsp olive oil

1 tbsp balsamic vinegar

100g Stilton cheese, crumbled

salt and freshly ground black pepper

Oil and heat a griddle pan until very hot. Add the asparagus spears and griddle until slightly charred and cooked through. Set aside.

Open out the chicken breasts, season and sprinkle both sides with the paprika. Place in the hot pan and griddle for 5–8 minutes on each side, until cooked through. Set aside.

Put the salad leaves in a bowl, add the grapefruit, onions, celery, cucumber, asparagus and pine nuts. Mix the oil and vinegar, season and pour over the salad. Toss well.

Slice the chicken diagonally and toss into the salad. Sprinkle with the Stilton and add a final grinding of black pepper.

CHICKEN, FENNEL *and* OUZO GRATIN

What a wonderfully comforting dish this is! I love the slightly aniseed flavour of the fennel and ouzo together, reminiscent of my years in Cyprus, and adapted to a cold British winter. Serve this with a crisp green salad and a sharp lemon vinaigrette.

Serves 4

butter, for greasing

200g cooked chicken breast, chopped

2 fennel bulbs, trimmed and quartered

½ baguette, cut into chunks

50g walnuts, chopped

For the cheese sauce

25g butter

25g flour

600ml milk

1 tbsp ouzo

1 tsp Dijon mustard

125g Gruyère cheese, grated

salt and freshly ground black pepper

Preheat the oven to 190°C/Gas mark 5. Butter a medium baking dish.

Cook the fennel in a pan of boiling water for 8 minutes. Drain and set aside.

To make the cheese sauce, melt the butter in a saucepan, then add the flour, stirring briskly to get rid of any lumps. Add the milk and gently bring to the boil, stirring all the time. Simmer for 10 minutes to cook out the flour. Remove from heat, stir in the ouzo, mustard and 100g of the cheese. Season to taste.

Arrange the chicken and fennel in the prepared dish and pour two-thirds of the cheese sauce over them. Spread the baguette chunks over the surface and sprinkle with the walnuts. Pour the rest of the sauce over the bread and sprinkle with the remaining 25g cheese. Season again and bake for 30 minutes, until golden brown and bubbling.

NORMANDY CHICKEN

From about the age of four I spent most of the school holidays in France visiting my godmother, Monique. She treated me as part of the family and I loved immersing myself in the French way of life. On one trip we visited Deauville in Normandy, and I vividly remember eating this light, creamy chicken dish followed by ginormous apple tarts for pudding.

Serves 4–6

600–700g chicken breasts

2 tbsp seasoned flour

dash of olive oil

75g unsalted butter

2 small onions, diced

2 garlic cloves, crushed

8–10 button mushrooms, halved

450ml medium-dry cider

1 bouquet garni

200ml crème fraîche

squeeze of lemon juice (optional)

salt and freshly ground black pepper

Put the chicken pieces in a shallow dish and coat them with the seasoned flour.

Heat the oil and butter in a flameproof casserole dish. Add the chicken and fry for 5–6 minutes, until brown on both sides. Transfer to a plate, then add the onions, garlic and the mushrooms and fry until tender. Return the chicken to the dish, add the cider, bouquet garni and crème fraîche, season and stir to combine. Once the liquid is bubbling, cover with a lid and simmer for about 20 minutes, until the chicken is cooked.

Using a slotted spoon, transfer the chicken to a warm serving dish. Discard the bouquet garni, then reduce the liquid in the casserole to the consistency of a sauce. Taste, then add some lemon juice and seasoning if necessary, and pour over the chicken. Serve with creamy mashed potatoes.

ASTI, ASPARAGUS *and* CHICKEN RISOTTO

I've been lucky enough to eat in some wonderful restaurants, and this dish is loosely based on a meal I ate at Gennaro Contaldo's several years ago. Asti gives a really great flavour to this risotto, but you can use any dry white wine. Note that using rosé will make the dish pink, but the taste will be just as delicious.

Serves 4–6

2 tbsp olive oil

1 large onion, finely chopped

500g chicken breast fillets, diced

500g Arborio rice

½ glass of Asti Spumante or any medium-dry white wine

250g asparagus, whole or chopped (depending on size)

1.2 litres warm fresh chicken stock

knob of butter

1 tbsp cream cheese

150g Parmesan cheese, freshly grated

2 tbsp chopped parsley

salt and freshly ground black pepper

Heat the oil in a heavy-based saucepan. When hot, fry the onion and chicken until the meat turns white but not browned.

Add the rice to the pan, stirring so that it is well coated in the oil. Pour in the Asti and stir now and then over a medium heat. When it has nearly evaporated, add the asparagus and just enough warm stock to cover the rice. Stir every so often over a medium heat until the liquid has been absorbed, then add more stock and repeat this process until the rice is tender and most of the liquid has been absorbed.

Take the pan off the heat and quickly stir in the butter, cream cheese and Parmesan. The risotto should have a loose, creamy texture – if it is too thick, add a little more stock.

Taste and season, garnish with the parsley, and serve with rocket and baby spinach salad.

Top left: somewhere in France stopping off to try the local food. Mummy, who spoke fluent French, would dash into a little bistro or restaurant to find out the price of the menu du jour – if it wasn't too expensive, we'd pile out of the car and sit and have a long, lazy and usually delicious lunch before setting off again. The journey was very much part of the holiday and along with my grandma we sampled a lot of bouillabaisse in southern France ... See recipe!

ROAST QUAIL *and* BEETROOT WITH A WARM LENTIL SALAD

I love beetroot, but my agent, Borra, made me promise not to do a beetroot and potato bake, so this recipe is for her. You can use poussins instead of quail; just make sure to use your fingers to get all the lovely meat off the bones.

Serves 4–6

4 small beetroot

4–6 quail

2 tbsp olive oil

1 small red onion, finely chopped

1 celery stick, chopped

250g ready-to-eat Puy lentils

150g goats' cheese

100g rocket leaves

salt and freshly ground black pepper

Preheat the oven to 200°C/Gas mark 6.

Wrap the beetroot loosely in foil and place in the oven for 40–50 minutes, until tender.

Season the quail, then heat the oil in a frying pan and brown them all over. Transfer to a roasting tray and roast for about 20 minutes, until tender. Set aside and keep warm.

Fry the onion and celery in the oil left in the pan until translucent. Set aside.

When the beetroot is cooked, remove from the oven and set aside until cool enough to handle. Peel off the skin and cut the flesh into chunks.

Heat the lentils according to the packet instructions. Add the onion, celery, rocket and beetroot, season well and stir to combine. Crumble the goats' cheese over the mixture, then place the salad on individual plates with the warm roast quail on top and devour!

CONFIT DE CANARD WITH RED WINE *and* BERRIES

OK, so it's canned duck preserved in its own fat, but if you can get your head around that, it really is the most delicious supper. It's one of those dishes you can throw together in less than half an hour, so it's ideal for unexpected guests (especially the ones who come with a bottle of wine in hand). I often buy large cans of confit when I go to France on holiday, but a lot of supermarkets sell them now, and they'll keep for ages in your cupboard.

Serves 4

1 large can confit de canard (4 legs)

¼ bottle (about 190ml) red wine

2 tsp cranberry sauce

2 tsp sweet chilli sauce

50g blueberries

50g redcurrants, on stems

handful of parsley, chopped

Variations: If you don't have fresh berries, use a little more cranberry sauce and a dash of port instead. Also, strawberry or blueberry jam can be used in place of cranberry.

Preheat the oven to 180°C/Gas mark 4.

Remove most of the fat from the duck legs, leaving just a light covering, and lay them in a roasting tray. Pour in the wine, then stir in the cranberry and chilli sauces. Sprinkle the blueberries and redcurrants all over the duck legs. Cover securely with foil and roast for 25–30 minutes, checking halfway through that the sauce is syrupy and not burning (add a little water if you're worried).

Transfer the duck to a warm serving dish. Spoon the excess fat off the sauce. Crush some of the berries into the sauce with the back of the spoon and pour over the duck. (No seasoning is needed because the duck is quite salty.) Garnish with the parsley and serve with garlicky mashed potato and salad.

Right: Me in Paris aged about 4–5 with my godmother, Monique. During the holidays I would be put on a plane to Paris and sent to stay with Monique, where I lived, spoke and ate like a little French girl. Many recipes, including the normandy chicken, my kitchen moules and my lavender-infused cheese boards come from my time spent with Monique.

RACK OF LAMB WITH A DIJON *and* PARMESAN CRUST

Here's another very easy dish that can be put together in minutes and is great fun to eat. Simply cut the racks into individual chops and you can nibble on them like lollipops – more good food that you can eat with your fingers, and lovely served with my Tartiflette (see page 204). I like my lamb to be pink in the middle, but if you prefer it well done, add another five minutes to the cooking time.

Serves 4

8-rib rack of lamb

For the crust

2 garlic cloves, finely chopped

25g Parmesan cheese, freshly grated

2 dried apricots, finely chopped

2 tbsp Dijon mustard

1 tsp finely chopped thyme

30g brown breadcrumbs

glug of olive oil

salt and freshly ground black pepper

Preheat the oven to 190°C/Gas mark 5.

Mix all the crust ingredients together in a bowl. Roll the rack of lamb in the mixture and place on a roasting tray, pressing more of the crust mix firmly on to the meat.

Roast for 25 minutes, and rest for 5 minutes before carving the rack into individual cutlets. Served with a salad of grilled halloumi, fresh figs and honey, or a big dish of Tartiflette (see page 204).

AUNTIE ALEX'S LASAGNE

I love having a house full of guests, and when we have friends or relatives to stay, the weekend usually turns into a sort of house party based around mealtimes. My nieces and nephews often request my lasagne to 'kick off' the weekend, and I'm only too happy to comply because it's so easy to do in large quantities. You can even prep it a day or so beforehand and store it in the fridge, ready to bake just in time for your guests' arrival.

Serves 6–8

2–3 tbsp olive oil

1 large onion, chopped

150g pancetta, chopped

3 garlic cloves, crushed

800g minced beef

150g minced pork

250ml red wine

2 x 400g cans chopped tomatoes

1 tsp sugar

1 tbsp tomato purée

handful of basil leaves, torn

1–2 bay leaves

1 Parmesan rind

75ml milk

butter, for greasing

8–12 dried lasagne sheets

80g Parmesan cheese, freshly grated

For the béchamel sauce

400ml milk

75g butter

75g flour

200ml double cream

1 small onion, halved

½ tsp nutmeg

salt and freshly ground black pepper

Heat the olive oil in a pan. When hot, fry the onions and pancetta for about 5 minutes. Add the garlic and stir for about a minute.

Add the beef and pork, using a wooden spoon to break them up, and cook on a high heat for another 8–10 minutes, until nicely coloured.

Add the wine, tomatoes, sugar, tomato purée, basil, bay leaves and Parmesan rind. Stir well, cover and simmer for about 1 hour. Every so often stir in a little of the milk until it has all been added. Remove the lid for the last 10 minutes of cooking time to reduce the liquid further. Discard the Parmesan rind.

Preheat the oven to 190ºC/Gas mark 5. Butter a medium ovenproof dish.

Meanwhile, make the béchamel. Heat the milk in a saucepan until almost simmering, then add the onion. Allow to simmer for 5 minutes, then set aside to cool slightly. Remove the onion and add the butter. When melted, whisk in the flour and return the pan to the heat, stirring constantly to avoid lumps forming. Cook out the flour for about 3–4 minutes, then add the cream and bring to the boil. Add the nutmeg, salt and pepper, then taste to check the seasoning and adjust as necessary.

Pour a layer of meat sauce into the prepared dish. Lay half the pasta sheets on top, overlapping them slightly. Pour one-third of the béchamel sauce over the pasta and spread to the edges of the dish. Sprinkle with some of the grated Parmesan, then repeat the layers in the same order, finishing with the béchamel and sprinkling with the grated Parmesan. Bake for 40–50 minutes, until golden and bubbling.

QUICK 'N' EASY CHILLI WITH CHOCOLATE *and* A TEQUILA SHOT

With most stews, the longer you cook them, the better they are, but with this fab little chilli, you can get away with a comparatively short cooking time and still produce a humdinger of a meal. The chocolate adds the same kind of richness and depth to the meat that you would normally get after an hour or more of cooking, while the tequila adds quite an unexpected punch.

Serves 4–6

2 tbsp olive oil

1 large onion, sliced

bunch of coriander, leaves picked and stalks finely chopped

1 garlic clove, crushed

575g lean minced beef

2 x 400g cans chopped tomatoes

2 tbsp tomato purée

2 tsp dried chilli flakes

1 x 400g can red kidney beans, drained and rinsed

1 cinnamon stick

1½ tsp cayenne pepper

30ml tequila

4 squares of dark chocolate (70–80% cocoa solids)

salt and freshly ground black pepper

To serve

soured cream

lime wedges

warm flatbreads

Heat the oil in a heavy-based saucepan or flameproof casserole dish. When hot, fry the onion, coriander stalks and garlic until softened. Add the beef and fry until browned.

Stir in all the remaining ingredients along with a handful of the coriander leaves. Season, then cover and simmer for 20 minutes. Remove the lid and cook for a further 10–15 minutes, until the liquid has reduced.

Serve the chilli sprinkled with the remaining coriander and dollops of the soured cream. Offer the lime wedges and warm flatbreads alongside.

BEEF CURRY WITH TOASTED CUMIN YOGHURT

I make this for my friend Dan, a serious 'curry fiend'. It's rich and spicy and is always a huge hit on curry nights. Serve with mountains of Coconut Rice and Peas (see page 203) and the Coconut Dhal with Mint and Coriander Chutney (see page 67).

Serves 4–6

3 tbsp olive oil

30g butter

2 large onions, sliced

3 garlic cloves, chopped

3 tsp chopped fresh root ginger

2 tsp mustard seeds

1 tsp ground turmeric

4 tsp medium curry powder

juice ½ lime

salt

1.5kg stewing beef, cut into chunks

4 large tomatoes, chopped

1 tsp tomato purée

1 tsp chilli flakes

2 hot red chillies, deseeded and chopped

6–8 Brazil nuts, crushed

handful of coriander leaves, to garnish

For the yoghurt

300g Greek yoghurt

4 tsp cumin seeds

salt and freshly ground black pepper

Heat the oil and butter in a heavy-based saucepan. When hot, add the onions, garlic and ginger and fry for a few minutes over a medium heat, until the onions start to colour.

Stir in the mustard seeds. As soon as they pop, add the turmeric and curry powder, and finally the lime and salt. Mix thoroughly.

Put the meat into the pan, stir to coat in the onion mixture and allow to brown over a medium heat.

Throw in the tomatoes, tomato purée, chilli flakes and chillies, reduce the heat, then cover and simmer for 1½–2 hours. Check occasionally to make sure the sauce doesn't dry out. If it looks like doing so, add a little water.

Meanwhile, make the yoghurt. Dry-fry the cumin seeds until they pop, then crush them using a pestle and mortar. Mix the powdered cumin into the yoghurt, season lightly and set aside untill needed.

When the meat is tender and the sauce rich and thick, taste and adjust the seasoning. Pour into a warm serving dish, sprinkle with the Brazil nuts and coriander. Serve with the yoghurt, plus the rice and dahl dishes suggested above.

Tip: This curry tastes even better if made the day before you plan to eat it, and that will save you time too.

Book club evening

Spicy chicken skewers with satay sauce | Mont d'or en croûte |
Baked Chinese duck with cucumber and chilli salad | Maison de la Roche
chocolate pudding cake

I reckon a book club is a perfect excuse to get together with like-minded people and eat some delicious food. In my opinion, some book clubs can take themselves a bit too seriously, and I don't like the formality of a full sit-down dinner while discussing what we've been reading. In my lovely long-standing club we read anything from Jilly Cooper to the classics, and the general rule, food-wise, is that whatever food we make must be simple to prepare and easy to nibble at or share. We take it in turns to host, and everyone brings a bottle. It's always a lovely evening and a great way to be introduced to books that you'd normally never read, or food you've not cooked before.

An oozing baked Mont d'or en Croûte (see page 118) served with a fresh crunchy salad is always popular when it's my turn to host. And my chicken satay (see page 117) is the perfect finger food. But, as with all entertaining, it's much more about the company than it is about serving up your finest dining, so don't feel under any pressure. If you can't get hold of Mont d'Or (aka vacherin), use a Camembert or Brie. Similarly, beef or prawns can be used instead of the chicken in the salad (see page 120), or fry some cubes of bread in a little oil, garlic and paprika for a vegetarian version. And if you have no time at all, just serve cut meats, cheeses and French bread with olives and nuts, and a little dish of olive oil with a splash of balsamic vinegar for dipping. Food and books — my two favourite things!

Spicy chicken skewers with satay sauce

This is a doddle to make and the perfect finger food. If you keep a range of spices, you can knock it up in no time, but if you don't quite have all the ingredients, you can simply make substitutions. No soy? Try Worcestershire sauce. Out of coconut milk? Use hoisin sauce or even tomato ketchup mixed with a little soy sauce and lime juice. No palm sugar? Try honey, brown sugar or even toffee sauce. Taste as you go and swap ingredients in and out whenever you need to. Have fun and experiment with the flavours.

Serves 4

4 chicken breasts, skinned and diced

For the marinade

2 tbsp smooth peanut butter

juice of 2 limes

1 tsp hot chilli sauce

4 tbsp dark soy sauce

3 garlic cloves, chopped

2 tsp finely chopped fresh root ginger

1 tsp medium-hot curry powder

1 tbsp palm sugar

1 tbsp sesame oil

For the sauce

2 tbsp crunchy peanut butter

2 tbsp coconut milk

1–2 tsp soy sauce

2 tsp sweet chilli sauce

1 tbsp sesame oil

1 tbsp water

1 tbsp lime juice

Put all the marinade ingredients into a large bowl and mix well. Add the chicken and turn to coat. Cover with cling film and leave in the fridge for a few hours.

Set out 8 skewers (if using bamboo ones, soak them in water for at least 30 minutes).

Preheat the grill until very hot, and cover the grill pan with foil.

Thread the chicken pieces on to the skewers and grill under a high heat for about 6 minutes on each side.

Meanwhile, combine all the sauce ingredients in a bowl. Divide the sauce between 4 little dishes and serve alongside each person's skewers.

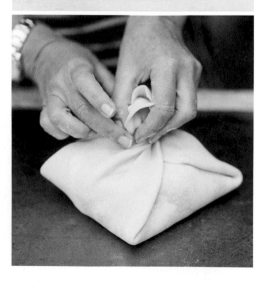

Mont d'or en croûte

If you love cheese as much as I do, this is the dish for you. Vacherin Mont d'or is a raw cow's milk cheese, beautifully runny with a strong, almost sweet flavour. Baking it wrapped in Serrano ham and concealed within a pastry case provides all the right elements for a match made in heaven. When cooked, the crisp and crumbly pastry gives way to the sweet and salty ham and there, in the middle, is the golden cheese oozing on to the dish. My mouth is watering just thinking about it! Stick it in the middle of the table so everyone can dip in.

Serves 4–6

flour, for dusting

250g ready-made puff pastry

4 slices of Serrano ham

1 ripe Mont d'or vacherin cheese

1 egg, beaten

Preheat the oven to 180°C/Gas mark 4. Line a baking tray with baking parchment.

Lightly flour a work surface and roll out the pastry to the thickness of a 50 pence piece. Using the rolling pin to help you lift it, place it on the prepared tray and chill in the fridge.

On a clean work surface, arrange the slices of ham on top of each other to form a 'Union Jack' star-shape: start by making a cross – 1 slice horizontal and 1 vertical; then place 2 slices on top in an x-shape. Place the cheese in the middle of the 'star', then fold the ham over, enclosing it completely.

Place the ham-wrapped cheese in the centre of the chilled pastry and wrap the pastry around it, cutting off the excess. Use the trimmings to make leaves to decorate the top of the 'parcel'. Ensure the pastry is well sealed and brush with the beaten egg. Bake for 35–45 minutes, until the pastry is golden brown. Serve with a light green salad dressed with vinaigrette, and some crusty bread.

Baked Chinese duck with cucumber and chilli salad

When I was younger I was transfixed by the shiny orange ducks hanging up in the windows of London's Chinatown restaurants. The spice rub they're coated with is gorgeously aromatic, and air-drying helps the flavours work into the meat. I've used the same method below, and the wonderfully intense flavour that results sits really well against the fresh, crisp cucumber.

Serves 6–8

6 duck breasts, skin scored with a diamond pattern

For the glaze

2 star anise

1 tsp ground cloves

2 garlic cloves

2 tsp ground cinnamon

75g cornflour

2 tsp freshly ground black pepper

2 tsp dark soy sauce

1 tsp ground ginger

2 tsp clear honey

zest of 1 orange

For the salad

1½ large cucumbers, peeled and chopped

1 large red chilli, deseeded and chopped

6 spring onions, sliced

handful of coriander leaves

pinch of salt

For the dressing

1 tbsp sesame oil

1 tsp honey

2 tbsp soy sauce

1 tbsp white rice wine vinegar or mirin

pinch of salt

Put all the glaze ingredients into a blender and blitz to a smooth consistency. Rub the duck breasts with the mixture, place on a tray and leave in a cool place for at least 2–4 hours.

Preheat the oven to 200°C/Gas mark 6 and preheat an oven tray.

Transfer the duck breasts to the hot tray and roast for 20–25 minutes. Set aside on a plate to rest for 5 minutes.

Meanwhile, put all the salad ingredients into a bowl. Combine all the dressing ingredients in a screwtop jar and shake well. Pour the dressing over the salad and toss.

Slice the rested duck breasts and serve on top of the salad.

Maison de la Roche chocolate pudding cake

One of my oldest friends, Honor, makes this for me when I stay with her in the south of France, where she runs a gîte business with her beautiful family and enormous dog, Bob. Our mothers were close friends when we were growing up, and would often cook together, and Honor and I have carried on that tradition in her big French kitchen with purchases from the local food markets. It's a perfect place to spend some time, and this is a perfect pudding!

Serves 8

120g unsalted butter, at room temperature, plus extra for greasing

250g dark chocolate

6 eggs

350g caster sugar

200g plain flour

icing sugar to finish

Preheat the oven to 200°C/Gas mark 6. Butter a 23cm heart-shaped cake tin.

Melt the butter and chocolate in a bowl set over a saucepan of simmering water (make sure the bowl doesn't touch the water).

Meanwhile, put the eggs and sugar into a bowl and whisk until light and fluffy. Stir in the flour.

Slowly add the melted chocolate and stir thoroughly to combine. Pour into the prepared cake tin and bake for about 25 minutes, until the top is firm but the middle still gooey (check by inserting a knife). Sprinkle some icing sugar over the top and serve warm with strong black coffee.

DRESSED-UP DINNERS

Nibbles | Bitter chocolate-dipped crisps with apple cider cocktails | Marinated olives with manchego cheese | *Starters* | Roast whole garlic and tomato soup | Baba ganoush with warm pitta bread | Potted crab with sourdough rounds | Prawn cocktail | Easiest-ever chicken liver pâté | *The Main Event* | Bouillabaise Mama Vanda | Coconut fish curry | Tarragon and mustard rabbit | Chicken in honey and orange | Sticky roast cardamom poussins | Lamb tagine with preserved lemons and olives | Preserved lemons | Flambéd fillet steak in brandy sauce | *After* | Cognac after-dinner truffles

To my mind, the words 'dinner party' always conjour up images of my mother in a maxi dress, my grandma in her peacock blue kaftan, a fabulously laid table sparkling with silver and candles, lots of pre-dinner nibbles and my dad in his cravat mixing aperitifs – Dubonnet rouge, Singapore slings and martinis. The food was always plentiful and it seemed extremely exotic to me – quiche lorraine, puffy vol-au-vents filled with chicken in a light white sauce, vichyssoise (my grandma's favourite), whole poached salmon cooked in my great-grandmother's fish kettle, beef stroganoff simmered slowly for hours on the old range oven, and the puddings … Mont Blancs (chestnut purée with brandy and sweetened cream), rum babas and syllabubs. I loved the theatre of it all. So now, when I do dress up, I like to recreate that slightly quirky 1970's feel at my own dinner parties.

With a little forethought you can avoid those horrible last-minute panics where you are standing hot-faced over the stove (not a great look) while your guests are having fun in the next room. If you take a little time to plan ahead, you'll be able to spend more time on important things, such as what you're going to wear. If you're worried about timings, skip the starters. Mix some fabulous cocktails and serve them with Chocolate-dipped Crisps (see page 131) or your own Marinated Olives and Manchego Cheese (see page 133). Your guests will love the personal touch, and they won't know it took five minutes to put together.

If you're feeling more confident or have fewer people to feed, impress them with the Flambéd Steaks (see page 153). Ask your guests how they like their meat cooked – it's surprisingly easy to get it right. Wherever possible, I will cook as much as I can the day before. The Lamb Tagine (see page 150) is perfect for this, as it actually tastes even better 24 hours later. Or you can cook the sauce from my Coconut Fish Curry (see page 144) and keep it in the fridge, adding the fresh fish just minutes before serving. The Potted Crab (see page 138) is a really simple starter that can be kept chilled until you are ready to serve, as can the Baba Ganoush (see page 137). And finish the meal with a deceptively simple decadent pudding, such as Heavenly Cherries with Hot Chocolate Sauce or Super-easy Lemon Syllabub in pretty individual glasses (see page 223 or 214).

Most important of all, however, is to remember that it's your evening too, so enjoy it! It's not about how fab your table looks, and it doesn't matter if some things turn out less than perfectly – it's *you* who makes the meal special. Put something of yourself into it and everyone will have a great time.

BITTER CHOCOLATE-DIPPED CRISPS WITH APPLE CIDER COCKTAILS

This is one of those ideas that shouldn't work, but it really does. Make sure you use really dark bitter chocolate and serve with a punchy cocktail. The ginger flavours in the apple cider cocktail work well with these crisps.

Serves 4–6

100g dark chocolate (85% cocoa solids)

1 large packet of ridged plain crisps

Place a heatproof bowl over a pan of simmering water, making sure the bowl and water do not touch. Break the chocolate into the bowl and allow to melt, stirring occasionally.

Line a baking sheet with greaseproof paper. Using a pair of tongs, dip each crisp halfway into the melted chocolate. Place on the prepared sheet and leave to set before serving.

KENTISH APPLE CIDER COCKTAILS

1 part vanilla vodka

2 parts medium sweet Kentish apple cider

1 part ginger beer

crushed ice

To garnish

mint leaves

cinnamon sticks (1 for each glass)

Combine the vodka, cider and ginger beer in a jug. Fill several jars or tall glasses with crushed ice, then pour in the cocktail. Garnish with mint leaves and a cinnamon stick.

I live surrounded by apple orchards and am a big fan of the local Kentish cider. I often serve this drink during the summer, in small jars with stubby straws.

MARINATED OLIVES WITH MANCHEGO CHEESE

These olives have a bit of a kick to them from the chilli flakes, so they're great served with aperitifs. Everyone will also be very impressed that you've marinated them yourself, and you needn't reveal that they took only a few minutes to knock up.

Serves 4–6

2 x 340g jars green olives, drained

100g Manchego cheese, chopped into chunks

6 black and pink peppercorns

4 large garlic cloves

2 sprigs of thyme

1 sprig of rosemary

2 bay leaves

150ml extra virgin olive oil

½ tsp chilli flakes

Place the olives and cheese in a bowl. Put the peppercorns and garlic into a mortar and crush with the pestle. Add the paste to the olives.

Crush the thyme and rosemary between your palms and mix into the olives, along with the bay leaves, olive oil and chilli flakes. Allow to marinate for at least 1 hour before serving.

Variation: Use any hard French cheese instead of Manchego.

ROAST WHOLE GARLIC *and* TOMATO SOUP

This soup is totally delicious. The garlic sweetens in its skin as it roasts and the balsamic heightens the aromatic flavour of the tomatoes. I always make double the amount then freeze it for later in the week for a special Sunday Supper.

Serves 4–6

1kg tomatoes (I often buy damaged reduced ones for this recipe)

1 garlic bulb, top sliced off

1 large carrot, peeled and chopped

2 celery stalks chopped

2–3 tbsp olive oil for drizzling

1tbsp balsamic vinegar

Handful of torn basil leaves for garnish 500ml fresh chicken stock (see page 18)

1 x 200g tub crème fraîche (optional)

salt and freshly ground black pepper

Preheat the oven to 190°C/Gas mark 5.

Cut the tomatoes in half and place them cut side up in a roasting tray. Slice the top off the garlic bulb then arrange it with the celery and carrots, between the tomatoes. Drizzle with the olive oil and the vinegar, season then cover loosely with foil and roast for about 1 hour.

When ready, squeeze the garlic cloves from the bulb into a food processor. Tip in everything else from the tray, including the juice. Add most of the basil leaves, reserving a few for garnish and blitz to a smooth consistency. Pour into a saucepan, add the chicken stock, season and heat through for a few minutes.

Serve with a dollop of crème fraîche (if using), a drizzle of olive oil and a final grind of black pepper. Don't forget to garnish with the reserved basil leaves.

BABA GANOUSH WITH WARM PITTA BREAD

As any of you who follow my Twitter feed will know, I love baked aubergine, and this is a classic dip made from it. The flavours are really warm and punchy, and it makes a great alternative to hummus. It can also be layered between slices of aubergine, tomato and courgette, topped with cheese and baked in the oven for a light midweek supper.

Serves 4–6

3–4 aubergines

½ tsp cumin seeds

1 tbsp olive oil

2 garlic cloves, crushed

125g tahini

juice of 1 lemon

handful of coriander leaves

4–6 pitta breads, cut into fingers

salt and freshly ground black pepper

Preheat the grill until very hot.

Prick the aubergines all over with a fork (this will prevent them from splitting when being cooked). Place on a tray under the grill and cook for about 20–30 minutes, turning occasionally, until the skin has charred all over. Set aside to cool.

Heat a heavy-based frying pan and dry-fry the cumin seeds until they pop. Crush to a powder using a pestle and mortar, then set aside.

Preheat the oven to 180°C/Gas mark 4.

Add the oil to the hot pan and gently fry the garlic until soft. Take off the heat.

Cut the aubergines in half lengthways and scoop out the flesh. Place it in a food processor with the garlic, tahini, lemon juice, crushed cumin, coriander leaves and seasoning and blitz to a rough paste. Transfer to a serving bowl, drizzle with a little more olive oil and add a sprinkling of black pepper.

Put the pitta slices on a baking sheet and warm in the oven until they start to brown at the edges. Serve with the baba ganoush.

POTTED CRAB WITH SOURDOUGH ROUNDS

Living quite close to the sea, I try to eat fish and shellfish whenever I can. Crab is a particular favourite of mine, and if I'm feeling particularly decadent, I might even make this for myself if I'm eating dinner alone. It's a really great starter for a dinner party because it can be made ahead, which means you can concentrate on the cocktails!

Serves 4–6

150g slightly salted butter
pinch of freshly grated nutmeg
juice of 1 lemon
285g fresh crabmeat
1 sourdough loaf, sliced
salt and freshly ground black pepper

To serve

butter cubes
lemon wedges

Melt the butter gently in a pan with the nutmeg and lemon juice. Season, then stir in the crabmeat and cook just for a minute or so.

Spoon the mixture into ramekins, gently patting it down, and chill for 2 hours before serving.

Toast the bread, then use a pastry cutter (any size you like) to stamp out circles. Alow to cool slightly and serve with the crab, butter cubes and lemon wedges.

PRAWN COCKTAIL

I really wasn't going to include this recipe until my husband expressed horror that his favourite starter was missing from my book. I suppose he has a point: every time I serve it up, it's always a huge hit, but for some reason no one can quite bring themselves to admit they love it. I say, embrace your appreciation of all things retro!

Serves 6

4 tbsp good-quality mayonnaise

2 tbsp crème fraîche

1 tsp sweet chilli sauce

2 tbsp tomato ketchup

1 tsp lime juice

splash of Tabasco sauce

600g cooked shelled prawns, drained

3 baby gem lettuces, finely chopped

2 pinches of cayenne pepper

handful of coriander leaves, chopped

salt and freshly ground black pepper

6 large cooked prawns, unshelled

Put 6 glasses to chill in the freezer.

Place the mayonnaise in a bowl and add the crème fraîche, chilli sauce, ketchup, lime juice, Tabasco and a little seasoning. Add the shelled prawns and mix well.

Get the glasses out of the freezer and place a little of the lettuce in each one. Pile the prawn mixture on top, then sprinkle with some of the cayenne, coriander and a little more ground black pepper. Finally, hang a whole prawn on the side of the glass and serve with wholemeal bread (see page 233) and butter.

At home with my sister Liz on Daddy's car! Groovy outfits, eh?

EASIEST-EVER CHICKEN LIVER PÂTÉ

My mother used to say, 'Every girl needs to have a chicken liver pâté recipe!' – definitely one of the great life lessons she handed down to me. Here's the quickest one in the whole world. Served with very thin slices of toast, it has a wonderful 1980's feel.

Serves 6–8

2 tbsp olive oil

2 onions, roughly chopped

2 garlic cloves, roughly chopped

450g chicken livers

knob of butter

1 tbsp brandy

pinch of freshly ground nutmeg

2 hard-boiled eggs, chopped

Heat half the oil in a frying pan. When hot, fry the onions and garlic until translucent. Transfer to a plate and set aside.

Chop the livers into small pieces, cutting out and discarding any white sinew. Add the remaining oil and butter to the empty onion pan and return to the heat. When the butter has melted, add the livers and cook until coloured outside but still pink inside. Do not overcook!

Add the brandy, then carefully tip the pan so that the brandy catches alight and flambés the contents. Once the flames have died down, add the nutmeg.

Stir in the reserved onions and garlic, then set aside to cool. When cooled, place in a food processor or blender and blitz to a coarse or smooth pâté, as you prefer.

Transfer the pâté to a bowl and stir in the chopped eggs. Cover and chill until needed.

Serve with brown toast circles (see page 138), placing them in a warm oven to dry a little before serving.

BOUILLABAISSE MAMA VANDA

On our family holidays we used to drive down to Spain through France, making sure we stopped off to sample regional dishes in some out-of-the-way little hotel or brasserie. When we got back home after one particular trip, my grandmother ingeniously recreated this rich fish stew from the south of France, and the flavours of orange, saffron, juicy tomatoes and shellfish always take me straight back to those happy holidays long ago.

Serves 4–6

4 tbsp olive oil

1 large onion, chopped

4 garlic cloves, crushed

1 leek, chopped

1 large red pepper, deseeded and sliced

1 x 400g can chopped tomatoes

1 tsp chopped oregano

1 bay leaf

1 tsp chopped fresh root ginger

3 strips of orange zest

2–3 drops of hot chilli sauce

900g monkfish, cod or haddock, boned and cut into thick chunks

300ml fresh fish stock

450g shellfish (e.g. prawns, scallops, mussels)

3 pinches of saffron strands

1 tbsp chopped coriander

salt and freshly ground black pepper

Heat the oil in a large flameproof casserole dish. When hot, add the onion, garlic, leek and pepper and fry gently until tender. Add the tomatoes, oregano, bay leaf, ginger, orange zest and chilli sauce, stir to combine, then simmer, uncovered, for around 10 minutes.

Add the monkfish and stock and simmer, uncovered, for a further 20–25 minutes.

Finally, add the shellfish and simmer for another 2 minutes. Season, sprinkle with the saffron and coriander and serve with sautéed potatoes or rice.

COCONUT FISH CURRY

Rich, creamy and unctuous, this is one of those great dinner party dishes that you can get a good head start on the day before. Make the sauce and keep it in the fridge, then add the fish just before you want to eat it.

Serves 4

1 tbsp sunflower oil

50g butter

1 large onion, finely chopped

1 tsp cumin seeds

200g canned chopped tomatoes

½ tsp chilli powder

½ tsp ground turmeric

1 tsp garam masala

2 green chillies, deseeded and chopped

1 x 400g can full-fat coconut milk

500g meaty white fish (e.g. cod, monkfish), cut into chunks

salt and freshly ground black pepper

To garnish

2 tomatoes, skinned, deseeded and chopped

handful of chopped coriander leaves

Heat the oil and butter together in a flameproof casserole dish. When hot, add the onion and cumin seeds and fry gently until translucent and fragrant.

Add the canned tomatoes, chilli powder, turmeric, garam masala and fresh chillies and cook for a further 5–8 minutes.

Pour in the coconut milk and bring to a simmer. Add the fish, then cover and cook for 15 minutes, until the fish is cooked through. Taste and season. Garnish with the coriander and fresh tomatoes, and serve with Coconut Rice (see page 203).

TARRAGON *and* MUSTARD RABBIT

Everyone seems to complain that they cook the same things night after night, so try something a bit different, such as game. If you give it a go and don't like it, I'll be amazed. Wild rabbits are surprisingly cheap to buy from butchers, but if you can't get hold of any, use chicken or pork instead.

Serves 4

3 tbsp flour

1 wild rabbit, cut into 4 pieces

50g butter

1 garlic clove, crushed

2 tbsp tarragon vinegar or white wine vinegar

150ml dry white wine

150ml water

150ml double cream

1 tbsp Dijon mustard

1 tbsp chopped tarragon leaves

salt and freshly ground black pepper

Season 2 tablespoons of the flour and dust the rabbit pieces with it. Melt the butter in a frying pan and brown the rabbit all over. Transfer to a warm plate.

Fry the garlic in the butter remaining in the pan for just a minute or so, then stir in the remaining tablespoon of flour until smooth. Gradually pour in the vinegar, stirring briskly and scraping up all the cooked bits from the bottom. Slowly pour in the wine, stirring as you do so, then allow to bubble for a few minutes to reduce slightly.

Return the rabbit to the pan, cover tightly with a lid and simmer gently for about 1 hour, until tender, adding the water if the meat becomes a little dry while cooking.

Lift out the rabbit and transfer to a warm serving dish. Stir the cream and mustard into the sauce and simmer uncovered for a few minutes to thicken slightly. Season to taste, then stir in the chopped tarragon. Serve with crusty bread and parsnip mash.

CHICKEN IN HONEY *and* ORANGE

I have a soft spot for combining sweet and savoury flavours, so when I had this dish at a dinner party held by an Algerian friend some years ago, I went straight home and wrote up what I thought was in the recipe. I've been cooking it ever since, but – depending on what ingredients I have – it always changes slightly. You can use lemons instead of oranges, or even satsumas, and maple syrup works well if you don't have any honey. The sticky caramelised orange pieces are delicious: eat them with your fingers, like it's half-time at a football match!

Serves 4–6

4 oranges, unpeeled and quartered

juice of 2 large oranges

2 cinnamon sticks

1 tbsp clear honey

½ tsp ground cinnamon

2 tbsp olive oil

1 small onion, finely chopped

8 assorted skinless chicken pieces (e.g. thighs, legs, breast on bone)

1 tsp ground ginger

1 tsp ground turmeric

1 tsp salt

freshly ground black pepper

sesame and/or poppy seeds, to garnish

Place the orange quarters and half the juice in a saucepan with 1 of the cinnamon sticks, the honey and cinnamon. Heat until the oranges start to caramelise slightly and the liquid becomes syrupy. If it reduces too much, add a little water, then set aside.

Meanwhile, heat the oil in a flameproof casserole dish and fry the onion until translucent. Add the chicken and the remaining cinnamon stick along with the ginger, turmeric, salt and pepper. Stir well and cook on a low heat for about 8–10 minutes, colouring all over.

Stir in the remaining orange juice and simmer, uncovered, for 20 minutes, or until the chicken is cooked through.

Season to taste, then transfer to a wide serving dish and arrange the caramelised orange segments over the chicken. Sprinkle with the sesame seeds and serve.

Variation: Try adding walnuts or almonds instead of the seeds.

STICKY ROAST CARDAMON POUSSINS

I am always amazed at how often I spot poussins on the reduced shelf in supermarkets. We only seem to want them for special occasions, but these small chickens are tender, quick to cook and each one is a perfect size for two people. This recipe is a bit of a hotch-potch of ingredients, but oh, boy, it is mouthwateringly good!

Serves 6

3 poussins, halved

2 tbsp walnut oil

4 tbsp tomato ketchup

20 cardamon seeds, crushed

1 red chilli, deseeded and chopped

juice of 1 lemon

1 tbsp honey

1 tbsp soy sauce

salt and freshly ground black pepper

Place the poussin halves in a dish. Put all the remaining ingredients in a screwtop jar and shake well. Pour the liquid over the birds, then cover and chill for at least 2 hours.

Preheat the oven to 180°C/Gas mark 4.

Transfer the birds and some of the marinade to a roasting tray and roast for 40 minutes, basting with the remaining marinade from time to time. The poussins are cooked when a skewer is inserted into the thickest part of the flesh and the juices run clear.

LAMB TAGINE WITH PRESERVED LEMONS *and* OLIVES

Such a wonderful dish, richly fragrant with the sweet spices and herbs of North Africa. You don't need one of those conical tagine dishes – a lidded casserole is fine – the point is to cook everything together very slowly so that the meat almost melts, the sauce ends up quite syrupy and you don't lose any of the lovely flavours or goodness.

Serves 6

1 large onion, roughly chopped

4 garlic cloves, chopped

2 carrots, cut into chunks

2 celery sticks, chopped into chunks

¼ tsp ground cinnamon

¼ tsp ground ginger

1 tsp ground turmeric

1 tsp ground cumin

1–2kg boneless lamb shoulder, cut into chunks

1 bay leaf

1 x 400g can chopped tomatoes

1 preserved lemon, quartered

1 x 340g jar pitted green olives, drained

1 tbsp harissa

1 tbsp honey

salt and freshly ground black pepper

coriander leaves, chopped, to garnish

Heat the oil in a large flameproof casserole dish. When hot, fry the onion, garlic, carrots and celery until browned. Sprinkle over the spices, then stir and fry for a further 2 minutes. Add the lamb, bay leaf and tomatoes, plus enough water to cover, then cover and simmer for 2 hours, until the lamb is tender.

Skim any fat from the surface. Add the lemon, olives, harissa and honey and cook, uncovered, for a further 5–8 minutes. Season generously and transfer to a serving dish. Garnish with the coriander and serve with couscous.

PRESERVED LEMONS

So easy to make, these lemons add an exotic Middle Eastern 'tang' to lamb, fish and pork and they look so pretty in the preserving jars, I often give them as presents too!

2 large kilner jars

8–10 large unwaxed lemons

350g sea salt (fine)

2–4 tbsp olive oil

2 tsp coriander seeds

2 tsp cumin seeds

2 tsp small dried chillies (optional)

2 tsp black or pink peppercorns

Sterilise the kilner jars by washing them in the dishwasher or clean with warm soapy water, rinse then dry in a warm oven. Cut each lemon with a cross, top and bottom, so that they are cut nearly to the middle but still stay whole. Sprinkle some salt in the bottom of each jar then pack in the lemons, sprinkling with more salt and the spices as you go. Push the lemons down firmly to leave a little space at the neck of the jar. Finish with the last of the salt and then fill the jar with cold water allowing a little space at the top but ensuring the lemons are totally covered. Pour in the olive oil, which acts as a seal, then close firmly and store in a cool dark place for at least 2 weeks before using.

FLAMBÉD FILLET STEAK IN BRANDY SAUCE

This is a perfect dish for a Friday night, when people are coming round straight from work. It's very simple, but is also a bit impressive and showy. I usually get everyone into the kitchen with me – glass in hand – while I get liberal with the brandy and they think I'm setting the kitchen on fire. If you don't have time to make anything much to serve with it, baked potatoes are a great accompaniment.

Serves 4

1 tbsp olive oil

50g butter

4 fillet steaks (about 150g each)

8 pink and black peppercorns

1 onion, finely chopped

100ml good-quality beef stock

4 tbsp brandy

300ml double cream

salt and freshly ground black pepper

Heat the oil with half the butter in a large frying pan. Meanwhile, season the steaks on both sides. When the butter has melted, fry the steaks for 4 minutes on each side (depending on thickness) if you want them medium rare. Give them another 30 seconds or so if you want them less rare. Transfer to a warm plate.

Melt the remaining butter in the pan, add the peppercorns and fry the onion until translucent.

Return the steaks to the pan, pour in the brandy and tilt the pan slightly so it catches alight. Stand back and allow the flames to die down, then remove the steaks again.

Pour in the stock, heat briskly to reduce by half, then pour in the cream. Leave to bubble and thicken, then season and stir. Pour the sauce over the steaks and serve with a green salad and a bottle of red – perfect!

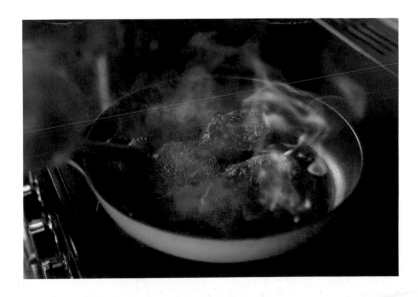

COGNAC AFTER-DINNER TRUFFLES

My sister Liz and I, aged four and eight, would help our grandma to make these lovely chocolates. Little hands are just the right size for rolling them, and we made them by the ton. Of course, as we made them, we'd furtively stuff them into our mouths and pockets, and emerge from the kitchen with cheeks like hamsters. My sister's truffles were always neater than mine, and even today she is much better at making sweet things than me.

Makes about 24

150g good-quality dark chocolate (80% cocoa solids)

25g butter

100g cake crumbs (buy a cheap sponge if you don't have any)

2–3 tbsp cognac

50g ground almonds

80g icing sugar

3 tbsp cocoa powder

Line a baking sheet with baking parchment. Place a heatproof bowl over a pan of boiling water, ensuring the bowl does not actually touch the water.

Put the chocolate and butter into the bowl and allow to melt together. Remove from heat and stir in the cake crumbs, cognac, almonds and 50g of the icing sugar. Take small spoonfuls of the mixture and shape them into little balls by rolling them between your hands. Place them on the prepared sheet.

Sift the remaining icing sugar on to one plate and the cocoa powder on to another. Roll half the balls in the sugar and the remainder in the cocoa powder. Keep chilled until you're ready to serve them with strong coffee.

Variation: Decorate the truffles if you like – with hundreds and thousands or chopped nuts.

LAZY SUNDAY LUNCHES

My dad's paella | Moroccan one-pot wonder | Pot au feu | Sausage and onion pie with English mustard | Simple roast pork with microwave apple sauce | Roast leg of lamb with juniper berries and red wine | Venison casserole with orange and ginger | Cottage pie with parsnip and parmesan crust | Spitfire beef stew with Kentish Cheddar and chive dumplings

There is something very special about Sunday lunch and most people have happy memories of them. When growing up, our Sunday lunches were all about large legs of lamb, joints of beef or giant meaty casseroles. There would be mountains of vegetables alongside, a cheeseboard afterwards and then pudding. Our labrador would sneak into the dining room between courses and hide under the table as close to my dad as possible, who would slip small slices of seriously stinky cheese into the waiting jaws below. In summertime we ate in the garden, feasting on a huge pan of paella made with fish, pork and rabbit, headily fragrant with saffron and paprika (see page 161). This was served with crisp salads, and poached fruits followed for dessert.

Nowadays, I like to think big and easy for long weekend lunches. If you can throw everything in one big pot or tray and leave it to cook slowly, you can enjoy more time with the family and friends you have invited over – plus, there's less washing up.

From spending time travelling and living abroad, I have developed a real love of Middle Eastern dishes, and over time have mixed up some of the iconic flavours with the more familiar recipes I learnt in France. The Moroccan One-pot Wonder (see page 164) is a favourite hotch-potch recipe, the original picked up when staying with a dear friend, George Brunet, in a tiny village called Paulmy in the Loire Valley. Back home I tweaked it to include some of those evocative flavours of Morocco – coriander, rose water, cumin and lemons – and cooked in the traditional way, slowly, making it a really simple but completely delicious lazy lunch.

I love the power that food has of bringing people together, to celebrate, to enjoy each other's company and to create new memories that last a lifetime. Keep it simple, keep it tasty and you can't go wrong.

MY DAD'S PAELLA

We would always spend the end of the summer holidays together as a family in southern Spain and travel home with a bootful of food and wine. We stopped off along the way if we saw food markets, and would choose little hotels to stay in according to the menu they advertised outside. My dad spent many years living in Madrid, so Spain had a special place in his heart. He adored Spanish food, and his paellas – using chicken, rabbit, prawns, mussels, squid and rich spicy chorizo to give depth to the flavour – were legendary. He would knock them up for parties in the garden with friends, or to have instead of a Sunday roast. Whenever I cook paella now it brings my father back into the room with me.

Serves 6–8

4 tbsp olive oil

1 large Spanish onion, sliced

3–4 garlic cloves, chopped

1 red pepper, sliced

1 green pepper, sliced

6 chicken thighs, skinned

100g bacon, diced

75g spicy Spanish chorizo

400g Arborio rice

1.25 litres Chicken Stock (see page 18)

100ml white wine

pinch of saffron or ½ tsp ground turmeric

1 tsp thyme leaves

1 tsp smoked paprika

3–4 large ripe tomatoes, chopped

200g baby squid, cut into rings (most supermarkets sell frozen squid tubes)

75g frozen peas

500g mussels, cleaned 500g mussels, cleaned

12 large prawns, peeled and deveined, but heads left on

handful of parsley, chopped

4 lemons, cut into wedges

salt and freshly ground black pepper

Heat the oil in a paella pan or large frying pan. When hot, fry the onion, garlic and peppers for a few minutes, until slightly softened. Add the chicken thighs and cook for about 10 minutes, depending on size, until nearly tender.

Add the bacon and chorizo, then stir in the rice, coating it in the oil, and cook for 2–3 minutes.

Pour in half the stock and half the wine, then stir in the saffron, thyme and paprika. Season and bring to the boil, then simmer for 15–20 minutes, stirring occasionally and checking to see if the rice is sticking. As the liquid reduces, stir in the remaining wine and stock. By this point the rice should be al dente.

Stir in the tomatoes, squid and peas, taste and season, and cook for a further 2–4 minutes. Tuck the mussels and prawns into the paella, cover with foil and cook for a further 5 minutes, until the shells open – discard any that remain closed.

To serve, sprinkle with the parsley and more freshly ground pepper, and dot the lemon wedges around the pan.

MOROCCAN ONE-POT WONDER

As I said in the introduction to this chapter, this dish is a bit of a hotch-potch of flavours influenced by my time spent in France and Morocco. It's really handy because you don't have to do anything while it's simmering away, and it will fill the house with its amazingly exotic aroma. Serve it up in the traditional way – on a big platter in the middle of the table with piles of warm pitta bread so that everyone can help themselves.

Serves 4–6

2 onions, quartered

1 leek, chopped

2 courgettes, roughly chopped

2 carrots, chopped into chunks

1 green pepper, deseeded and chopped

¼ butternut squash, chopped into chunks

6 small waxy potatoes

3 celery sticks, roughly chopped

1 medium chicken

1 tsp ras el hanout

1 tsp ground turmeric

6 prunes

1 x 400g can chopped tomatoes

2 tbsp tomato purée

1 tbsp olive oil

juice of 1 lime

1 tsp honey

salt and freshly ground black pepper

2 tbsp toasted flaked almonds (see page 30), to garnish

Preheat the oven to 190°C/Gas mark 5.

Throw all the vegetables into a large roasting tray and sit the chicken on top. Sprinkle with the ras el hanout, turmeric, salt and freshly ground black pepper, then dot the prunes around.

Put the tomatoes into a bowl, add a canful of water, the tomato purée and oil and stir to combine. Carefully pour the mixture over the chicken and vegetables. Squeeze the lime juice all over, then cover tightly with foil and cook for for 1½–2 hours, removing the foil for the last 15 minutes. Test for readiness by piercing the thickest part of the chicken with a skewer; it is done when the juices run clear. Transfer the chicken and vegetables to a warmed serving plate.

Place the roasting tray on the hob and add the honey to the liquid, plus a little more seasoning if necessary. Reduce over the heat until syrupy, then pour over the chicken. Garnish with the toasted almonds and serve.

POT AU FEU

Here's a real family favourite, and something I cook at least once a month. Traditionally made with beef or oxtail, I prefer to use a whole chicken. After simmering it for a couple of hours, I then blitz the sauce to a rich, thick broth – perfect with crusty French bread and a crisp green salad. If there are any leftovers, add lentils and a dash of créme fraîche to make a hearty soup. Nothing gets wasted in my kitchen.

Serves 4–6

1 tsp olive oil

1 large onion, roughly chopped

3 large garlic cloves, chopped

1 x 120g packet lardons, or 3 rashers of streaky bacon, chopped

2 celery stalks, roughly chopped

150g baby carrots, roughly chopped

1 large parsnip, roughly chopped

1 x 1.8kg chicken

2 tbsp Sauternes or any other sweet white wine

1 tsp dried mixed herbs

2 bay leaves

salt and freshly ground black pepper

handful of parsley, chopped

Heat the oil in a large flameproof casserole dish. When hot, fry the onion, garlic and lardons until the onion is translucent and the lardons browned.

Add the vegetables and fry briskly until soft and golden. Push them aside in the pan and place the chicken beside them, breast down. Fry on both sides until brown.

Turn the chicken breast-side up on top of the vegetables, pour in the Sauternes and allow to evaporate a little. Sprinkle the herbs all over, add the bay leaves, then pour in enough water to nearly cover the chicken. Season, cover and simmer very gently for about 2 hours, until the chicken is completely cooked through. Transfer the bird to a warm serving dish.

Discard the bay leaves from the casserole dish, then scoop out about two-thirds of the vegetables and blitz them to a purée. Skim most of the fat off the sauce remaining in the pan, then stir in the puréed vegetables. Taste and season accordingly.

Pour the sauce over the chicken, garnish with the chopped parsley and serve with crispy rosti potatoes.

SAUSAGE *and* ONION PIE WITH ENGLISH MUSTARD

As it can be made ahead and kept in the fridge overnight or even frozen, this pie is ideal for a Sunday gathering (just make sure you defrost it fully before you reheat it). It's really important to use good-quality sausages with a high meat content because they take centre stage in this dish. You can use flavoured sausages, but I like to keep it simple for a good old-fashioned English lunch. Serve with my Horseradish Mash and Homemade Gravy (see pages 202 and 21). Any leftovers can be eaten cold the next day, like a pork pie.

Serves 6–8

oil, for frying and greasing

2 large onions, chopped

1 large garlic clove, crushed

800g good-quality pork sausages (or buy sausage meat if your butcher is good)

4 sage leaves, chopped

1 tbsp freshly chopped parsley

2 tsp English mustard powder or paste

2 eggs, beaten

flour, for dusting

salt and freshly ground black pepper

For the pastry

300g plain flour

150g salted butter, cubed

1 egg yolk

pinch of salt

2–3 tbsp water

First make the pastry. Put the flour and butter into a bowl and rub together with your fingers until the mixture looks like fine breadcrumbs. Stir in the egg yolk and salt, then use a knife to gradually mix in the water until a dough forms. Bring it together with your hands, then wrap in cling film and chill.

Preheat the oven to 190°C. Grease a shallow medium pie dish.

Heat a little oil in a frying pan. When hot, fry the onions and garlic until golden. Set aside.

Strip off the sausage skins and put the meat into a bowl. Add the onion mixture, the sage, parsley and mustard and mix together with a wooden spoon. Season well, then stir in half the beaten egg.

Lightly dust a work surface with flour and roll out the pastry to the thickness of a 50 pence coin. Use to line the prepared dish. Trim the edges and fill the pastry case with the sausage and onion mixture. Brush the rim of the pie dish with the second beaten egg.

Reroll the pastry trimmings to form a lid, place over the whole pie and trim off any excess. Using finger and thumb, pinch the pastry edges closed all the way around, like a pasty. Cut a little hole in the centre, then reroll the trimmings and cut out leaf shapes to decorate the top.

Brush the surface of the pie with the remaining beaten egg and bake for 30–40 minutes, until golden outside and bubbling inside. Serve with large dollops of Horseradish mash and a glass of cider.

SIMPLE ROAST PORK WITH MICROWAVE APPLE SAUCE

You can't beat a classic roast. I think most people would probably choose chicken or beef, but I love roast pork – especially the crackling. It's Paul and Josh's favourite too. Any leftovers can go into the Porky Burgers or be mixed with beef and made into meatballs (see pages 82 or 85).

Serves 8

2 onions, quartered

1 x 2kg loin of pork

2 tbsp olive oil

1–2 tsp flour

125ml white wine

salt and fresh ground black pepper

For the apple sauce

225g cooking apples

50g butter

½ tsp lemon zest

50ml water

1 tsp caster sugar, or to taste

Preheat the oven to 180°C/Gas mark 4.

Place the onions in a roasting tray. Using kitchen paper, pat the pork skin as dry as possible. Now take a very sharp knife and score the skin and fat (not the meat itself) diagonally in a diamond pattern. Rub the oil all over the skin and into the cuts. Sprinkle generously with salt and pepper, then place the joint on top of the onions. Roast for 2 hours and 35 minutes.

Meanwhile, make the apple sauce. Peel, core and slice the apples. Place them in a microwavable dish and add the butter, lemon zest and water. Cover with cling film, leaving a corner open for steam to escape, and heat on High for 8–10 minutes. Check to see if the apples are soft enough to mash. If not, give them another 4–5 minutes. Mash them to the desired texture, add the sugar to taste and set aside until needed. (If you don't have a microwave, simmer the ingredients instead in a small saucepan, mashing them up with the back of a spoon.)

Transfer the cooked joint to a warm meat plate, cover loosely with foil and set aside to rest for at least 20 minutes.

Place the roasting tray on the hob, spoon off most of the fat and any burnt onion, but keep the caramelised bits. Pour in the wine and stir well to scrape up any bits sticking to the pan. Increase the heat, add 150ml of water (ideally from the vegetables you are cooking to serve with the meat), then quickly stir in the flour to avoid lumps forming. Cook, stirring constantly, for a few minutes. Season and pour into a gravy boat to offer alongside your pork and crackling. Serve the roast with Tartiflette (see page 204) and you have a culinary marriage made in heaven.

ROAST LEG OF LAMB WITH JUNIPER BERRIES *and* RED WINE

Although this recipe takes about five hours to cook, you don't actually have to be around to keep an eye on it, so it's ideal if you have a houseful of guests. I usually do a big cooked brekkie to sustain everyone for a long walk or trip to the beach, and the exercise works up an appetite for later.

Serves 6

2–3 tbsp olive oil

2.5kg leg of lamb

1 head of garlic, cut in half horizontally

2 onions, roughly chopped

2 carrots, roughly chopped

200ml red wine

150ml water

handful of rosemary leaves

3–4 juniper berries

1 tsp redcurrant jelly

juice of ½ lemon

salt and freshly ground black pepper

Preheat the oven to 160°C/Gas mark 3.

Heat the oil in a large roasting tray on the hob. Season the lamb and put it in the tray for a few minutes, turning so that it colours and seals all over. Set the joint aside.

Add the garlic, carrots and onions to the oil remaining in the tray and toss them over the heat until well coated. Add the wine, heat until bubbling, then simmer for a few minutes, until the onion starts to become translucent. Remove from the heat and place the lamb on top of the vegetables. Add the water, sprinkle on the rosemary, some more seasoning and the juniper berries. Cover tightly with thick foil (you don't want any of the steam to escape), them place in the oven for 4–5 hours, basting occasionally. When cooked, tranfer the lamb to a meat plate and keep warm.

Skim the fat from the tray, then scrape all the juices and lovely sticky bits into a sieve set over a bowl. Push them through with the back of a wooden spoon, then return the contents of the bowl to the roasting tray. (Discard any solids left in the sieve.) Add the redcurrant jelly and lemon juice a bit at a time, tasting as you go to reach the flavour you want, then adjust the seasoning if necessary. Heat the gravy through and serve with the lamb. Baked fennel with lardons is a lush accompaniment!

VENISON CASSEROLE WITH ORANGE *and* GINGER

For some unknown reason, venison is another one of those meats that I often find on the reduced shelf in the supermarket, and when I do, I snap it up and stick it in my freezer. It's low in fat yet richly flavoured, and is fantastic in this stew – another dish you can leave cooking slowly for a long time while you get on with reading the Sunday papers.

Serves 6–8

30g butter

1 tbsp olive oil

150g smoked lardons

1kg stewing venison, cut into chunks

3 tbsp flour, seasoned with salt

2 onions, chopped

2 garlic cloves, chopped

1 tsp chopped fresh root ginger

500g tomatoes, chopped

1 tsp dried thyme

2 bay leaves

½ tsp allspice

1 cinnamon stick

250ml beef stock

50ml port

100ml orange juice

200g turnips, chopped

200g parsnips, chopped

200g baby carrots

salt and freshly ground black pepper

chopped parsley, to garnish

Heat the butter and oil in a large flameproof casserole dish. When hot, fry the lardons until crispy. Using a slotted spoon, transfer them to a plate.

Coat the venison in the seasoned flour, then brown the meat in batches and set aside with the lardons.

Now fry the onions and garlic until translucent. Return the venison and lardons to the pan, then add the ginger, tomatoes, herbs, spices, stock, port and orange juice. Season, stir well, then cover and simmer for 1 hour. (If the mixture becomes a little dry, add a splash of water.)

Add the vegetables and cook for a further hour, removing the lid for the last 10 minutes.

Taste and adjust the seasoning, then discard the cinnamon stick. Garnish with the parsley and serve immediately with crusty sourdough.

COTTAGE PIE WITH PARSNIP *and* PARMESAN CRUST

Parsnips have a lovely sweetness that I just can't resist. In autumn this makes a really comforting and filling dish, and it's easy to double up if you have more people to feed than usual. Serve it with buttered bread for anyone who is particularly hungry.

Serves 6–8

2 tbsp olive oil

2 onions, chopped

2 carrots, chopped

2 celery sticks, chopped

1kg minced beef

1 tbsp Worcestershire sauce

200g baked beans

½ bottle Rioja or any other hearty red wine

pinch of ground cinnamon

1–2 tsp gravy granules

1 tsp tomato purée

2 bay leaves

small handful of parsley, chopped

800g potatoes, chopped

400g parsnips, chopped

125ml milk

1 tbsp soured cream

40g butter

30g Parmesan cheese, freshly grated

1 egg, beaten

salt and freshly ground black pepper

Preheat the oven to 180°C/Gas mark 4.

Heat the oil in a large frying pan. When hot, fry the onions, carrots and celery until translucent. Add the mince and fry until browned. Stir in the Worcestershire sauce and the beans, then add the wine, cinnamon, gravy granules, tomato purée and bay leaves and simmer, covered, for about 20–30 minutes, until the liquid has reduced slightly.

Remove the bay leaves, add the parsley, then tip the mixture into a deep ovenproof dish and set aside.

Cook the potatoes and parsnips in boiling salted water until tender. Drain and place both in one saucepan. Add the milk, cream, butter and seasoning, then mash until smooth. Stir in the Parmesan followed by the egg.

Using a large spoon or spatula, spread the potato over the meat mixture, taking it right to the edges of the dish. If you wish, use a fork to mark a criss-cross pattern on the top. Using the handle of the fork, make a small hole in the centre of the potato for the steam to escape.

Place the pie in the centre of the oven and bake for 30–40 minutes, until the top is golden brown and bubbling. Serve with green beans or a light salad with a mustard dressing.

SPITFIRE BEEF STEW WITH KENTISH CHEDDAR *and* CHIVE DUMPLINGS

Beer and beef make a winning combination in this casserole, and the fluffy dumplings nestled on top really complete the dish. My great-grandmother was the cook in a big London house at the turn of the century, preparing lavish dinner parties, but also making homely food, such as dumplings, a skill she passed down through the generations. Spitfire beer is brewed locally to us in Kent by some friends of ours, and has a great subtle flavour. You don't have to use Spitfire, of course, but make sure you go for a fairly pale ale, as anything stronger can be a bit overwhelming.

Serves 4–6

2 tbsp sunflower oil

3 onions, sliced

800g stewing beef cut into bite size chunks

1 tbsp flour

300ml Spitfire beer or other pale ale

1 tsp muscovado sugar

pinch of ground cinnamon

salt and freshly ground pepper

For the dumplings

125g self-raising flour

50g shredded suet

30g strong Kentish Cheddar cheese, grated

1 tsp chopped chives

3 tbsp water

Preheat the oven to 160ºC/Gas mark 3.

Heat the oil in a flameproof casserole dish. When hot, fry the onions until golden. Add the beef and brown it all over. Sprinkle in the flour and stir well to combine, then pour in the beer. Add the sugar and cinnamon, season generously and mix well. Cover with a lid and cook for 1½–2 hours, until the beef is tender and falls apart easily. Check midway through cooking to ensure the stew doesn't become dry; if it does, just add a little water.

To make the dumplings, put the flour and suet in a bowl, add the cheese and chives, season well and mix together. Slowly stir in the water to form a loose dough. Divide the dough into 6–8 equal pieces and roll them into balls. Arrange them on top of the stew about 20 minutes before the end of cooking time, then return to the oven, leaving the lid off. Serve with baked potatoes and Roast Baby Carrots with Cumin (see page 196).

Summer Lunch in the Garden

Butterfly lamb with mint, feta and balsamic marinade | Crab, Cheddar and watercress quiche | Pissaladière | Lavender honey cheeseboard | Poached peaches with fresh raspberry cream

As soon as the weather gets a bit warmer, I love to get everyone together so that we can eat outside. Even if we all have to wear an extra jumper, I won't waste an opportunity! It doesn't matter what your table looks like after a winter of being bashed about by the wind and rain – just spread a big cloth over the top, put out some tea lights in jam jars and no one will know.

I find you can get more people over if you're sitting outside as they can squeeze in on mismatching chairs and stools, or stand around with drinks in their hand, and the kids can all go off and play, while you linger through the afternoon into the evening. There's something truly magical and very relaxing about eating in the garden, and the food you serve should be just as fuss-free and enjoyable to make.

Prepare a few simple dishes, such as the Crab, Cheddar and Watercress Quiche or Pissaladière (see page 181 or 182), that you can put in the middle of the table for everyone to help themselves, and serve with salads and vegetables (see pages 188–207) and lots of crusty bread. Also, be sure to cook extra so that as the day turns to evening, your guests can come back for more to nibble on and keep the party going.

Butterfly lamb with mint, feta and balsamic marinade

We eat a lot of lamb here in Kent, and this is a gorgeous summer recipe. Its tangy balsamic and mint marinade cuts through the slight fattiness of the meat. Serve with Roast Vegetable Couscous or Crushed Baby Potatoes (see page 207 or 199).

Serves 6–8

1 x 1.75kg leg of lamb, boned and butterflied (ask your butcher)

juice and zest of 1 lemon

3 garlic cloves

8 tbsp good-quality balsamic vinegar

150ml olive oil

5 tbsp chopped mint

2 tbsp muscovado sugar

75g feta cheese

salt and freshly ground black pepper

Open out the leg of lamb and push 2 long skewers through the meat to hold it in the butterfly shape.

Put the lemon juice and zest in a large shallow dish, add the garlic, vinegar, oil, mint, sugar and seasoning and mix well. Lay the meat in the dish and baste with the oil mixture. Cover and set aside to marinate for a couple of hours, or leave overnight in the fridge.

Preheat the oven to 180°C/Gas mark 4.

Place the meat on a rack in a roasting tray, reserving the marinade, and roast for 25–30 minutes on each side. Baste from time to time with the reserved marinade. The meat should remain pink in the middle.

Carve the lamb into slices and arrange them on a warm meat plate. Crumble the feta over them and sprinkle with a little black pepper. Serve with Roast Vegetable Couscous or a Radish and Orange Salad (see page 207 or 44).

Crab, Cheddar and watercress quiche

My sister and I grew up by the sea and used to go crab fishing, bringing our catch back to the kitchen, where it would be popped into a saucepan and cooked for supper. Crabmeat is versatile and delicious, and when combined with strong Cheddar and fresh watercress, as it is in this quiche, it makes a divine summer lunch with a green salad.

Serves 6–8

200ml double cream

2 eggs plus 2 egg yolks

50ml crème fraîche

1–2 tsp freshly ground nutmeg

1 tbsp chopped chives

pinch of cayenne pepper

350g fresh crabmeat

bunch of watercress, roughly chopped

2 tbsp grated Cheddar cheese

salt and freshly ground black pepper

For the pastry

125g plain flour, plus a little extra for dusting

75g butter

pinch of salt

Preheat the oven to 180°C/Gas mark 4. Grease a loose-bottomed 23cm tart tin.

To make the pastry, put the flour, butter and salt into a food processor or bowl and process or rub together until the mixture resembles breadcrumbs. Add a tablespoon of water at a time, mixing until a dough forms.

Lightly flour your work surface and roll out the pastry. Use to line the prepared tin, then cut off the excess with a sharp knife. Line the pastry case with baking paper, fill with baking beans or rice and chill for 15 minutes.

Bake the chilled case for 8–10 minutes, then remove the beans and paper and bake for a further 6–8 minutes. Set aside and lower the oven to 160°C/Gas mark 3.

Gently warm the cream in a saucepan. Meanwhile, put the eggs, extra yolks and crème fraîche into a bowl and whisk together. Slowly pour this mixture into the warm cream, stirring gently. Add the nutmeg, chives, cayenne and seasoning, then stir in the crabmeat, watercress and most of the cheese. Pour the mixture into the pastry case, sprinkle the remaining cheese over the top and bake for 35–40 minutes, until golden brown.

Pissaladière

My mother made this French-style pizza again and again whenever we had parties, sleepovers or picnics. And no matter how much she made — however many trays were stacked up — there would never be any left! I remember my eighteenth birthday and the garden table groaning under the weight of all the food. There was a crowd of my friends, cans of beer and dodgy white wine in one hand and slices of pissaladière in the other — perfect!

Serves 6

flour, for dusting

375g ready-made puff pastry

1 tbsp olive oil

knob of butter

1kg onions, thinly sliced

1 garlic clove, crushed

1 bouquet garni (sprigs of rosemary, parsley and thyme tied together)

2 large tomatoes, skinned and chopped

16 anchovy fillets, drained

30 pitted black olives

salt and freshly ground black pepper

Preheat the oven to 180°C/Gas mark 4.

Lightly flour a work surface and roll out the pastry to fit a 25 x 38cm baking sheet and leave a 2cm overhang. Turn in the overhang to make a rim all around the edge.

Heat the oil and butter in a flameproof casserole dish. When hot, add the onions, garlic and bouquet garni and fry very gently for about 20 minutes, stirring every so often until the onions are sticky, translucent and golden.

Add the tomatoes and cook for another couple of minutes, then discard the bouquet garni. Season and stir, then spread the mixture over the pastry.

Arrange the anchovies in a criss-cross pattern over the surface, then dot the olives all over the top. Bake for 25–30 minutes, until golden brown.

Lavender honey cheeseboard

I adore cheese, and this cheeseboard brings back so many memories for me: as a child in the south of France with my godmother; on holiday with my family in the Loire; or, more recently, with my husband and son, staying with my dearest friend, Honor, in her beautiful farmhouse gîte. The warm, ripe flavours of the cheese are complemented perfectly by the aromatic, summery sweetness of the honey and figs. Delicious!

Serves 6

200g clear honey
1 tbsp freshly picked lavender flowers
crottin de chèvre (young goats' cheese)
Époisses (cows' milk cheese washed in brandy)
Figs to serve

Put the honey and lavender in a heatproof bowl and microwave gently until hot, but do not allow to boil. Alternatively, heat gently in a small saucepan. Cover and allow to infuse for up to 1 hour. It will depend on the strength of your lavender, so taste a little every so often: you want a good 'kick' of lavender flavour. When ready, pour the mixture through a fine sieve, discarding the lavender.

Pour the honey into a screwtop jar and allow to cool before replacing the lid. Store in a cool place.

When ready to serve, place the cheese on a board and cut into slices. Pour the lavender honey into a ramekin and serve on the board along with freshly cut figs and forks for dipping.

Poached peaches with fresh raspberry cream

Peaches, golden and sunny, taste headily of summer. Here they are poached in vanilla and sugar syrup, then topped with raspberry cream – heaven! This was one of my grandmother's favourite recipes; she was very keen on poached fruit, which often came straight from the garden, and she always added a generous glug of alcohol for good measure.

Serves 6

4–6 ripe peaches

250g caster sugar

1 tsp vanilla extract

several fine strips of lemon zest

300g fresh raspberries

175ml crème fraîche

1 tbsp framboise liqueur

Place the peaches in a saucepan and pour boiling water over them. Cover and leave to sit for a minute or so, then drain and peel – the skin should come off easily. Cut the peaches in half, remove the stones and return the fruit to the pan, adding just enough water to cover them.

Add about 200g of the sugar, the vanilla and lemon zest. Bring to the boil, then simmer for 6–8 minutes, until the peaches are tender and the liquid syrupy. Transfer to a bowl and chill.

Push the raspberries through a sieve to remove the seeds. Whip the crème fraîche into soft peaks, then fold in the raspberry mixture, framboise liqueur and remaining sugar. Serve chilled with the poached peaches.

and

ginger & blackberry chocolate brownie trifle p212

EAT YOUR VEGETABLES

French beans with thyme and pancetta | Stir-fried garlic courgettes |
Roast baby carrots with cumin and maple sauce | Cauliflower cheese
with mozzarella and nutmeg | Griddled asparagus with almonds and
Roquefort | Crushed baby potatoes with mint and sea salt | Ratatouille |
Horseradish mash | Coconut rice with peas | Tartiflette | Roast vegetable
and toasted almond couscous

I adore vegetables and think they should be celebrated in all their glory, given a central role at mealtimes, not shuffled to the side of the plate as an afterthought. Give me a big bowl of pasta mixed with Stir-fried Garlic Courgettes (see page 195), a squeeze of lemon juice, a little black pepper and some Parmesan shavings – plus a glass of chilled wine – and that's my idea of perfection.

Vegetable dishes don't need to be complicated, but they do need to be interesting. Think of them on their own – do they look tasty? If not, why not? I'm not a food snob and will happily cook with frozen veg, canned veg, even those dodgy-looking veg from the reduced shelf. It takes only a splash of olive oil, some chopped chives or a little garlic butter melted over the top to turn the most unappealing carrot, for example, into a joy to behold.

Ratatouille (see page 200), brought to the table in a large, colourful dish, its bubbling Parmesan crust calling out to be eaten, is always a winner at Sunday lunch. I serve it with simple roast beef or garlic-studded lamb and it makes a lovely change from traditional greens. French Beans with Thyme and Pancetta (see page 192) are irresistibly aromatic and utterly delicious with Pepper-blackened Salmon (see page 77). And my son's favourite, Crushed Baby Potatoes with just a little salt, melting butter and chopped fresh mint (see page 199), is so tasty, you could eat it all on its own.

As with all my recipes, those in this chapter are all a bit mix-and-match and very accommodating if you find yourself lacking in one thing or another. If you don't have Roquefort, for example, use feta or Parmesan, or leave it out altogether. No pancetta? Use chopped bacon. Out of walnuts? Try toasted almonds. Don't like horseradish in your mash? Add mustard or a little garlic oil instead. The only hard-and-fast rule here is never to overcook your veg – they'll not only lose all their goodness, but will end up soggy and flavourless. Also remember to keep in mind the balance of flavours so that you don't overpower their natural subtleties.

Taste as you go and have fun jazzing up and making these dishes your own. Vegetables are most definitely not boring!

FRENCH BEANS WITH THYME *and* PANCETTA

Green beans are at their best when cooked very simply — just lightly steamed, maybe with a little garlic and crème fraîche, a squeeze of lemon and some seasoning. The recipe below is more of a wintry dish, and so delicious that I could almost eat it on its own, maybe adding some Parmesan croutons to oomph it up.

Serves 8

800g French beans

60–80g pancetta

1 tsp chopped thyme

2 shallots, finely chopped

30g butter

salt and freshly ground black pepper

Top and tail the beans, then cook them in a pan of boiling water for 4–6 minutes, until they are just tender. Drain and set aside.

Heat a dry frying pan until hot, then quickly brown the pancetta. Stir in the thyme, then transfer the mixture to a plate.

Fry the shallots in the fat remaining in the pan. When translucent, add the butter, the pancetta mixture and beans. Stir well, taste and season, and serve straight away.

STIR-FRIED GARLIC COURGETTES

A fantastically versatile side dish, this goes with almost anything, or it can be tossed through penne or rigatoni with a squeeze of lemon, a twist of black pepper and a little Parmesan for a quick pasta sauce.

Serves 4–6

1 tbsp sunflower oil

4–6 courgettes, sliced into discs about 1cm thick

1 garlic clove, crushed

1 tbsp water

pinch of sugar

squeeze of lemon juice (optional)

salt and freshly ground black pepper

Heat the oil in a large frying pan. When hot, quickly fry the courgettes until they start to brown. Stir in the garlic, then the water, sugar and a pinch of salt. Continue frying until the courgettes are tender.

Transfer to a dish, sprinkle with pepper and a squeeze of lemon juice, and serve.

ROAST BABY CARROTS WITH CUMIN *and* MAPLE SAUCE

The maple syrup really brings out the sweetness of the carrots here, but use honey or brown sugar if you prefer. I also make this dish with parsnips, grating over a little lemon zest just before serving.

Serves 6

600g baby carrots
1 tbsp sunflower oil
1 tsp cumin seeds
30g butter
2 tbsp maple syrup
salt and freshly ground black pepper

Preheat the oven to 180°C/Gas mark 4.

Put the carrots and oil in a roasting tray, season and mix well. Roast for 20–30 minutes, until blistered and tender.

Dry-fry the cumin seeds in a small saucepan until they pop, then add the butter and maple syrup. Heat until bubbling.

Mix the cooked carrots with the sauce, transfer to a dish, season and serve.

CAULIFLOWER CHEESE WITH MOZZARELLA *and* NUTMEG

My whole family loves cauliflower cheese, and whenever my Auntie Sylvia comes to visit, she always requests this for supper. I use a lot of cheese in this recipe because I think the sauce should be really thick and luxurious, trailing great strings of mozzarella when you spoon it out. This is definitely rich enough to eat as a meal in itself with just a crisp side salad.

Serves 6

500ml milk

1 small onion, cut in half

1 bay leaf

25g butter

25g plain flour

1 tsp Dijon mustard (optional)

generous pinch of nutmeg

75g medium Cheddar cheese, grated

50ml double cream

1 cauliflower

1 mozzarella ball

2 slices of stale bread, made into breadcrumbs

salt and freshly ground black pepper

Preheat the oven to 180°C/Gas mark 4.

Put the milk, onion and bay leaf in a saucepan, bring to a simmer, then remove from the heat and leave to infuse for about 10 minutes. Discard the onion and bay leaf and let the milk cool slightly.

Melt the butter in a saucepan, then stir in the flour and gently sizzle the mixture for a couple of minutes. Take the pan off the heat and gradually whisk in the milk. Return to the heat and bring to the boil, continuing to whisk to avoid lumps forming, then simmer for 8–10 minutes, stirring occasionally. Add the mustard (if using) and the nutmeg, then stir in the Cheddar and cream, and add some seasoning.

Discard the cauliflower leaves and stalk, then cut the head into largish florets. Cook in a pan of boiling water for about 4 minutes, until just tender. Drain and transfer to an ovenproof dish.

Pour the cheese sauce over the cauliflower, then grate the mozzarella over the top. Sprinkle with the breadcrumbs and bake for 15–20 minutes, until golden and bubbling.

GRIDDLED ASPARAGUS WITH ALMONDS *and* ROQUEFORT

Asparagus has a very short season, but when it is around, you should eat it whenever you can. This is another veggie dish that I sometimes eat as a light salad on its own or with a poached egg and a generous sprinkling of black pepper on top.

Serves 4

30g flaked almonds, toasted (see page 30)

1 tsp olive oil

250g young asparagus

freshly ground black pepper

50g Roquefort cheese (optional)

Heat a griddle pan and drizzle with the oil. Meanwhile, bend each asparagus spear until it snaps and discard the woody ends. Griddle the spears for a couple of minutes, until tender and slightly charred all over.

Place the asparagus in a warm serving dish, season with black pepper, crumble the Roquefort over them and sprinkle with the toasted almonds. Serve warm.

CRUSHED BABY POTATOES WITH MINT *and* SEA SALT

New potatoes need very little extra added to them. Here the mint and salt bring out the lovely sweetness of their skins.

Serves 4–6
750g Jersey Royal potatoes
30g slightly salted butter
10g mint, chopped
sea salt flakes and freshly ground black pepper

Cook the potatoes in a pan of boiling water until just tender. Drain and set aside.

Melt the butter in the empty pan, add the potatoes and salt flakes, and shake the pan over the heat until the butter becomes slightly brown and nutty in flavour.

Take the pan off the heat and use a fork to gently crush the potatoes. You want to keep the texture, so don't overdo it and mash them.

Stir in the mint, check for saltiness, then add a little black pepper and serve.

RATATOUILLE

A real childhood favourite – I remember huge dishes of ratatouille being brought to the table to eat with slices of garlicky roast lamb or rib of beef. The cheesy breadcrumb topping gives it a wonderful crunchy, oozy crust that everyone will fight over.

Serves 6–8

4 tbsp olive oil

2 large onions, sliced

4 garlic cloves, crushed

1 red pepper, deseeded and chopped

4 courgettes, sliced into discs 1cm thick

2 large aubergines, cut into chunks

2 tsp dried herbes de Provence

2 x 400g cans chopped tomatoes

1 tsp sugar

handful of basil leaves, torn

generous handful of brown breadcrumbs

2 tbsp grated Parmesan cheese

salt and freshly ground black pepper

Heat the oil in a heavy-based saucepan. When hot, fry the onions, garlic and red pepper until slightly caramelised.

Add the courgettes and aubergines and fry quickly for a minute or so. Stir in the herbes de Provence, then the tomatoes, sugar and some seasoning. Keep over a high heat until the mixture bubbles, then simmer gently for 30–40 minutes, until the sauce becomes syrupy and the vegetables are tender. Stir in the basil leaves and check the seasoning. Transfer to an ovenproof serving dish.

Heat the grill until hot. Meanwhile, put the breadcrumbs and Parmesan into a bowl, mix well, then sprinkle the mixture all over the ratatouille. Pop under the hot grill for 5–8 minutes, or until the topping is bubbling and golden. Serve straight away.

HORSERADISH MASH

I've given classic mashed potatoes a bit of a kick in this recipe by adding a little horseradish. Taste it as you go and use only as much as you like because horseradish can be quite fiery. Finish with a good twist of black pepper.

Serves 6

1.5kg potatoes, quartered
75g butter
30g crème fraîche
4 tsp creamed horseradish
100–150ml whole milk
salt and freshly ground black pepper

Cook the potatoes in a large pan of boiling water until tender. Drain and mash.

Mix in the butter, crème fraîche and horseradish, then gradually stir in the milk, adding just enough to achieve your preferred consistency. Season and serve.

Variations: Use a big dollop of Dijon mustard instead of horseradish for a milder and slightly sweeter flavour. Alternatively, add a splash of garlic oil – not too much, as you don't want it to be greasy. (If you don't have garlic oil as such, fry a couple of unpeeled garlic cloves in olive oil until hot but not sizzling. Allow to cool, then squeeze out the garlic, mix it with the oil, then whisk the mixture into the mash.)

COCONUT RICE WITH PEAS

Adding coconut milk to rice gives it a really creamy texture and flavour – a bit like Thai rice. This recipe is also a great way of getting an extra veg into your meal without anyone really noticing. Feel free to add anything else you like to the rice; peppers and courgettes are also good. It goes perfectly with my fiery Beef Curry (see page 110).

Serves 4–6

1 tbsp vegetable oil

1 small onion, finely chopped

300g basmati rice (rinsed)

400ml coconut milk

400ml water

400g frozen peas, cooked until tender

handful of chopped coriander

salt and freshly ground black pepper

Heat the oil in a pan. When hot, fry the onion until translucent.

Rinse then add the rice and stir to coat in the oil. Pour in the coconut milk and water, mix well and bring to the boil. Cover and simmer until the rice is cooked and the liquid has been absorbed.

Stir in the peas and coriander, then season and serve.

TARTIFLETTE

Having worked in the Alps for five years, I got to know tartiflette – a hearty and extremely rich potato dish – very well. It uses a wonderful gooey and flavourful cheese called reblochon, but you can use whatever cheese you like. I sometimes make a big batch of tartiflette and, when it has cooled, slice it into portions and freeze it. For a tasty fuss-free supper, I put it in a dish with a bit more cream, cover it with foil and reheat it at 180°C/Gas mark 4 until it's bubbling. Delicious served with baby spinach leaves.

Serves 6

butter, for greasing

1 garlic clove, halved

oil, for frying

1 onion, chopped

1 x 120g packet smoked lardons

1 tsp dried thyme

2kg waxy potatoes, cut into 2cm chunks

125ml white wine

1 tbsp Kirsch or brandy (optional)

500g chilled reblochon cheese

400ml double cream

salt and freshly ground black pepper

Preheat the oven to 180°C/Gas mark 4. Butter a large ovenproof dish and rub the garlic all around the inside.

Fry the onion and lardons, until they become caramelised, then add the thyme. Scrape the mixture into the prepared dish, then add the potatoes and mix well. Season generously. Add the wine and the Kirsch (if using).

Scrape off the red wax disc on the underside of the reblochon, then cut the cheese into thinnish slices. Lay them across the potatoes, covering as much of the surface as possible.

Pour the cream all over and bake for 1–1½ hours, until the cheese is crusty and bubbling and the potatoes are cooked through.

Tip: Using the cheese straight from the fridge makes it easier to slice.

ROAST VEGETABLE *and* TOASTED ALMOND COUSCOUS

Couscous is a wonderful ingredient, and a very worthy store-cupboard staple. It is a great carrier for all sorts of vegetables, meats and herbs, and a substantial meal or side dish can be put together in a matter of minutes. I often fry up leftovers from a Sunday roast or our dinner the night before, and add to couscous with a good balance of spices to create a quick and tasty garden lunch. Use what you have and the variations on this dish are endless.

Serves 4–6

2 red onions, quartered

1 red pepper, deseeded and quartered

1 green pepper, deseeded and quartered

2 courgettes, cubed

1 aubergine, halved and cubed

1 sweet potato, cut into bite-sized cubes

1 tbsp olive oil, plus an extra dash for the dressing

4 garlic cloves, left whole

1 tsp cumin seeds

¼ tsp ground cinnamon

350g couscous

450ml hot Chicken or Vegetable Stock (see page 18)

1 large knob of butter

zest and juice of 1 lemon

3 tbsp chopped mint

salt and freshly ground black pepper

50g toasted flaked almonds (see page 30), to garnish

Preheat the oven to 190°C/Gas mark 5.

Place all the cut vegetables in a roasting tray and mix in the oil, garlic, cumin, cinnamon and seasoning. Roast for 40–45 minutes, then cover with foil and set aside.

Put the couscous in a saucepan and pour in just enough stock to cover it (add a little more boiling water if necessary). Set aside for 10 minutes, then add the butter and fluff up with a fork.

Put the lemon zest and juice into a screwtop jar with a dash of oil, the mint and seasoning and shake well.

Combine the vegetables with the couscous and dressing in a serving dish. Sprinkle over the almonds and serve.

Variation: If you don't have stock, use water and then fork through an additional large knob of butter just before serving.

PUDDINGS *and* DESSERTS

Ginger and blackberry chocolate brownie trifle | Super-easy lemon syllabub | Rice pudding perfection | Kevin Post's cobbled plums | Blueberry bakewell tart | Strawberry and lemon curd meringue roulade | Roast pineapple with homemade custard | Heavenly cherries in hot chocolate sauce | Rhubarb crumble ice cream | Apple tartski

I have a sweet tooth – I admit it – and will readily miss a restaurant starter to make sure I have enough room for the most luscious dessert on the menu.

Puddings were a must when I was growing up. I think my mother and grandmother were in secret competition as to who could produce the most delicious dessert. Rich and fluffy chocolate mousses made with eggs, cream and brandy vied with traditional baked cheesecakes, queen's pudding made with homemade strawberry jam, and delectable strudel. My sister and I would watch in fascination to see how thin Mum could roll out the pastry on my great-grandma's rickety old kitchen table. She always got it almost transparent, before rolling it up with apple, dried fruit and spices. Then she dusted it with icing sugar and baked it until crisp and fragrant. Later, when it was dished up, we'd watch eagle-eyed to make sure neither one of us got a larger serving than the other!

I love making giant Apple Tartski (see page 226), a recipe I picked up when I was a chalet girl. It's sweet and sticky but the crème fraîche cuts through the richness. Roast Pineapple with Homemade Custard (see page 222) is also a big hit in our house, and no one can resist a slow-baked Rice Pudding (see page 214), eaten warm from the oven and fragrant with nutmeg.

And don't forget about using up pudding leftovers. Crumble tart or roulade remnants into whipped cream or custard, then freeze to make ice cream. You can do the same with uneaten poached fruits or the Heavenly Cherries cooked in wine (see page 223). Also, a little cold rice pudding with warm pears and a chilled glass or Marsala is a real treat the next day. As you can see, pudding leftovers are incredibly versatile – provided there are any!

GINGER *and* BLACKBERRY CHOCOLATE BROWNIE TRIFLE

This is possibly the easiest trifle to throw together and was the result of a clear-out of my larder and fridge. Fiery ginger chocolate and sharp blackberries are perfect companions for the sticky sweetness of the brownies and the generous amounts of cream and mascarpone used as a topping. It's a seriously decadent pudding. You can use canned fruit (try cherries) if you don't have fresh, and swap the ginger for a glug of kirsch. It works beautifully with shop-bought choccy muffins too.

Serves 6

2 x 100g bars Green & Blacks ginger chocolate

350ml double cream

1 tbsp Greek yoghurt

400g mascarpone cheese

1 quantity Brownies (see page 61), broken into bite-sized chunks

1–2 tbsp ginger wine

250g fresh blackberries

50g good-quality dark chocolate (80% cocoa solids)

50g toasted flaked almonds (see page 30)

Melt the ginger chocolate in a heatproof bowl placed over a saucepan of boiling water (make sure the bowl doesn't touch the water), then set aside to cool slightly.

Whip the cream into soft peaks, then fold in the yoghurt.

Beat the mascarpone into the cooled melted chocolate.

Arrange half the brownies in the bottom of a pretty bowl or glass jug. Sprinkle with a little of the ginger wine, then layer half the blackberries, half the chocolate mixture and half the cream on top. Repeat these layers and use the back of a spoon to 'peak up' the top layer of cream.

Grate the dark chocolate over the surface and sprinkle with the almonds. Keep chilled until serving.

SUPER-EASY LEMON SYLLABUB

Like ice cream, syllabub is traditionally served cold, but is nowhere near as heavy. This is my great-grandma's recipe, perfect for grown-up dinners and family lunches. It's refreshingly light and delicious, and everyone will scrape their bowl clean.

Serves 6

2 tbsp caster sugar

zest and juice of 2 lemons

500ml double cream

1–2 drops vanilla extract

Put the sugar and lemon juice into a bowl and stir until the sugar has dissolved.

Whip the cream into soft peaks, add the vanilla, then gently fold in the sugared lemon juice and the zest.

Pour the syllabub into glasses and chill until needed. Serve with warm Oven Shorties (see page 238).

RICE PUDDING PERFECTION

There is something very comforting about rice pudding eaten piping hot with a dollop of homemade jam or preserves in the middle – ginger preserves are especially lovely – or served chilled with poached fruits. It's unctuously delicious and quite irresistible. This pudding takes a little longer to cook than usual, but if you pair it with a slow-cooked dish (such as the Venison Casserole on page 171), you can go off for a long walk to work up your appetite.

Serves 6

30g unsalted butter, plus extra for greasing

1.2 litres full-fat milk

140g pudding rice

2 drops of vanilla extract

55g caster sugar

pinch of ground nutmeg

Preheat the oven to 140°C/Gas mark 1. Butter a large ovenproof dish.

Pour the milk into a saucepan and bring to a simmer. Add the rice, vanilla and sugar, stir well and pour into the prepared dish. Sprinkle with the nutmeg and dot with the butter. Bake for 1½ hours, stirring halfway through.

KEVIN POST'S COBBLED PLUMS

For years we have shared Christmas, Easter, birthdays and anytime meals with our great friends Helen and Kevin Post, who live near us. Helen even handed over her legendary lemon drizzle cake recipe to Paul for his book! Not to be outdone, Kevin – a serious wine buff – 'assisted' me with testing the different variations of fortified wine to complement the plums in this great cobbler recipe ... hic!

Serves 6

850g plums, halved and stoned
1 tbsp orange juice
4 tbsp Marsala wine
100g light muscovado sugar
2 tbsp water
icing sugar, for dusting

For the cobbler topping

200g self-raising flour
100g lightly salted butter
1 tsp baking powder
100g caster sugar
100–120ml full-fat milk

Preheat the oven to 190°C/Gas mark 5.

Place the plums in an ovenproof dish. Pour the orange juice and Marsala over them, sprinkle with the muscovado sugar and finally the water.

To make the cobbler topping, put the flour, butter and baking powder into a food processor or bowl, and process or rub together until the mixture resembles breadcrumbs. Add the caster sugar and mix again. Pour in the milk a little at a time, mixing until a soft dough forms. Place spoonfuls of the dough on top of the fruit, then bake for 30–35 minutes, until thoroughly cooked.

Dust with icing sugar before serving, and serve with dollops of vanilla ice cream.

BLUEBERRY BAKEWELL TART

We eat a lot of blueberries in the Hollywood household. I use them in sauces, jams, cakes and even in stews. They work really well in wintry dishes, especially those using venison or duck (see page 171 or 105). However, this tart has to be one of my favourite blueberry recipes. If I have some, I use my own Homemade Jam in it (see page 234), which I'm sure makes it taste all the more special. Ridiculously simple to make and using mainly ingredients you're likely to have in your cupboard, the tart is perfect for afternoon tea in the garden or after an impromptu supper.

Serves 8

100g unsalted butter, plus extra for greasing

flour, for dusting

500g ready-made shortcrust pastry

4 eggs

100g caster sugar

100g ground almonds

50g flaked almonds

2 tbsp blueberry jam

175g blueberries

Preheat the oven to 190°C/Gas mark 5. Butter a 24cm loose-bottomed tart tin.

Lightly flour your work surface and roll out the pastry to the thickness of a 50 pence coin. Use to line the prepared tin, then trim off the excess. Chill for 20 minutes.

Prick the bottom of the pastry case with a fork, line it with baking parchment and fill it with baking beans or rice. Beat one of the eggs in a small bowl, then brush it around the rim of the pastry and bake for 10 minutes. Remove the parchment and beans and bake the case for a further 5 minutes, until golden brown.

Put the butter and sugar in a saucepan and heat until dissolved. Pour into a bowl and beat in the 3 remaining eggs. Stir in both the ground and flaked almonds.

Spread the jam inside the pastry case, add the blueberries and pour the almond mixture over the top. Bake in the centre of the oven for 20 minutes.

Set the tart aside to cool in the tin, then transfer to a serving dish. Serve warm with clotted cream and a cup of Earl Grey tea.

STRAWBERRY *and* LEMON CURD MERINGUE ROULADE

Meringue roulade is one of those puddings that, no matter how it seems to turn out, always looks and tastes mouthwateringly good. Sharp lemon curd against sweet strawberries and cream, all mixed together with the sticky, almost toffee-like meringue ... need I say more?

Serves 6–8

5 large eggs, separated

250g caster sugar

1 tsp cornflour

1 tsp white wine vinegar

50g toasted flaked almonds (see page 30)

icing sugar, for dusting

300ml double cream

200g fresh lemon curd

400g strawberries, hulled and chopped

small handful of mint, chopped

Preheat the oven to 140°C/Gas mark 1. Line a baking sheet with baking parchment.

Put the egg whites into a large bowl and whisk until stiff peaks form. Fold in the caster sugar a spoonful at a time, then fold in the cornflour. Stir in the vinegar. Spread the mixture into a rectangle on the prepared baking sheet. Sprinkle the almonds evenly over the surface and bake for about 45 minutes, until the meringue is starting to brown. Switch off the oven and leave the door ajar while the meringue cools inside. When cold, invert it on to a sheet of greaseproof paper sprinkled with the icing sugar.

Pour the cream into a clean bowl and whip until thick.

Spread the lemon curd all over the meringue. Cover with the cream, then arrange two-thirds of the strawberries on top. Roll up from the short side, using the paper to help you.

Transfer the roulade to a plate and sprinkle with the remainder of the strawberries, then the chopped mint. Dust with icing sugar and serve.

ROAST PINEAPPLE WITH HOMEMADE CUSTARD

Why is it that so many people seem to avoid fresh pineapples in shops and supermarkets and make do with canned? Maybe it's the preparation that puts them off, so I've added a tip that makes it easier. Fresh pineapple is bursting with flavour, utterly delicious and my son adores it. I particularly like it roasted in the oven so that it caramelises and becomes even sweeter. Adding a dash of rum enhances its tropical flavour, and it's fantastic served with huge helpings of homemade custard.

Serves 4–6

2 tbsp rum

2 tbsp fresh orange juice

150g light brown sugar

pinch of cinnamon

1 vanilla pod, split open lengthways

1 large pineapple, peeled and cored (see tip below)

30g butter, cubed

For the custard

150ml full-fat milk

200ml double cream

1 vanilla pod split lengthways, or 1–2 tsp good-quality vanilla extract

4 large egg yolks

50g caster sugar

Preheat the oven to 190°C/Gas mark 5.

Heat the rum, orange juice and sugar in a small saucepan, stirring until the sugar has dissolved. Add the cinnamon and vanilla, then set aside.

Chop the pineapple into large chunks and place in an ovenproof dish. Pour the rum mixture all over it and dot with the butter. Bake for 30 minutes, until the pineapple is soft. Check halfway through, and if the liquid is evaporating too quickly, add a splash of water.

To make the custard, put the milk, cream and vanilla in a saucepan, bring just to the boil, then remove from the heat.

Put the egg yolks and sugar in a bowl and whisk until frothy. Continuing to whisk, slowly pour the milk mixture into the egg yolks. Return the liquid to the saucepan and stir over a low heat until it begins to thicken. Remove the vanilla pod (if used) by straining the custard into a jug. Serve with the roast pineapple.

Tip: To prepare a fresh pineapple, slice off the leaves and base. Stand the pineapple on its base and slice the peel downwards, sawing it away in strips. To remove the 'eyes', make v-shaped cuts on either side of them, continuing the cuts diagonally so that you end up with a spiral channel all the way around the fruit. Cut out and discard the woody core, then use the fruit as required.

Variation: Any liqueur, brandy or whiskey can be used instead of the rum, or you can just leave out the alcohol entirely.

HEAVENLY CHERRIES IN HOT CHOCOLATE SAUCE

This is a dish I remember well from my childhood. Both my French godmother and my mother were keen to use up any remnants of red wine in their cooking, and if it didn't end up in gravy, it appeared in pudding. The alcohol cooks off in this dish, so you are left with the lovely, fruity flavours of the wine, the treacly taste of port and, of course, the lush, fresh cherries. Top it with hot chocolate sauce and you'll be in heaven…

Serves 4

600g cherries, stoned

100g sugar

½ bottle of Chinon red wine, or anything you have open

2 tbsp port

1 vanilla pod, split open lengthways

For the sauce

100g mini marshmallows

100ml double cream

75ml runny honey

50g dark chocolate (80% cocoa solids)

pinch of salt

Place the cherries, sugar and alcohol in a pan. Scrape in the vanilla seeds and and add the pod too. Bring to the boil, then simmer for 20 minutes or so.

Using a slotted spoon, transfer the poached cherries to a bowl. Turn up the heat and reduce the liquid to a lovely thick syrup.

Discard the vanilla pod, then pour the syrup over the cherries and set aside.

To make the sauce, place all the ingredients for it in a heavy-based saucepan and heat gently, stirring constantly until the marshmallows and chocolate have completely melted.

Serve the cherries warm or chilled with the chocolate sauce.

RHUBARB CRUMBLE ICE CREAM

My mother is the queen of ice cream! Every summer she loads her freezer with different flavours — raspberry, white chocolate and meringue, strawberry, chocolate and nougat, brown bread, pistachio … the list is endless, and so is the queue waiting outside the kitchen door for her latest creation. She uses an ice-cream machine these days, but this recipe doesn't need one.

Makes 1 litre

500g forced rhubarb, trimmed and cut

100g caster sugar

pinch of ground cinnamon

350ml double cream

200g condensed milk

For the crumble

100g flour

75g unsalted butter

75g soft brown sugar

50g porridge oats

2 drops of vanilla extract

Place the rhubarb in a saucepan with the caster sugar, cinnamon and just enough water to cover them. Bring to the boil, then simmer until the rhubarb has softened.

Using a slotted spoon, transfer the rhubarb to a dish, then simmer the liquid in the pan until thick and syrupy. Pour it over the rhubarb and set aside to cool. When cold, blitz the rhubarb to the consistency of thick jam.

Preheat the oven to 160°C/Gas mark 3.

Meanwhile, make the crumble. Put the flour and butter in a bowl and rub them together with your fingers until the mixture resembles breadcrumbs. Add the sugar, oats and vanilla and stir to combine. Spread the crumble mix over an oven tray and bake for about 15 minutes, until golden brown, stirring halfway through. Set aside to cool.

Whisk the cream and condensed milk together until soft peaks form. Fold in the rhubarb mixture, followed by all but 1 tablespoon of the crumble. Pour into a plastic container and sprinkle the reserved crumble over the top. Cover and freeze for 8 hours. Serve in cones or with shortcake biscuits.

APPLE TARTSKI

While working as a chalet girl in the French Alps, I learnt that this take on the classic tarte Tatin was a must for all chalet dinner parties. After a hard day's skiing, everyone loves the sticky, sweet apples in a light pastry case with dollops of crème fraîche. I always put in a shot of génépi, the Savoyarde mountain liqueur, but go easy, though – it'll knock your socks off!

Serves 6–8

flour, for dusting

500g puff pastry

4–6 strong, crisp apples (e.g. Granny Smiths, Pink Ladies)

160g apricot preserve

2 tbsp génépi (or any other liqueur you like – elderflower is a good substitute – but you could use brandy, calvados or even tequila)

100g light brown caster sugar

35g unsalted butter, cubed

icing sugar, for dusting

Preheat the oven to 200°C/Gas mark 6. Line a baking sheet with baking parchment.

Light flour a work surface and roll out the pastry to the thickness of a £1 coin. Lay it on the prepared baking sheet, then fold in the overhang to form a rim. You will need to make tucks in it at regular intervals as you work your way around the edge. Chill the pastry for 10 minutes.

Meanwhile, peel and core the apples, then chop them into slices about as thick as a 50 pence coin. Cover the chilled pastry with the apple, overlapping the slices as you go.

Put the apricot preserve and the génépi in a saucepan and heat until the jam has melted. Pour the mixture over the apples, then sprinkle with the caster sugar and dot the butter around. Bake for 35–40 minutes, until the pastry and apples start to turn golden brown. (I often stick mine under a hot grill at the end to get it well caramelised.) Dust with a little icing sugar before serving.

Afternoon tea

My hubby's perfect loaf recipe | Homemade summer berry jam | Anchovy butter | Smoked salmon and dill butter | Oven shorties | Strawberry and white chocolate rocky road | Grandma's fruitcake | Raspberry chocolate bombes

I have fantastic memories of the afternoon teas put on by my extremely glamorous grandmother. She would drive down to see us at the weekend from her house in London and set up a cake stand, tea tray and china cups in the garden. As a small child, there was something wonderfully magical about the whole event. There had to be two types of tea (Earl Grey and lapsang souchong), a cake or cream sponge, fruit loaf and buttered toast fingers spread with Gentleman's Relish.

After-school teatime at home was a far simpler affair. Ravenous, we would consume slices of homemade bread lavishly spread with butter and dollops of Homemade Jam (see pages 233 and 234), followed by biscuits, such as the shortcake on page 238, filled with raisins and pecans, or buttery oatmeal cookies.

These days everyone is just so busy that afternoon tea seems to have taken a bit of a back seat, but, given the choice between dinner in a flashy restaurant or afternoon tea on the lawn of a slightly antiquated hotel, tea would win hands down with me every time. As a dedicated fan of afternoon tea, I've had a few amazing ones at hotels around the country, and as a family we often take time to revisit them.

In your own surroundings you might not be able to have croquet on the lawn or achieve the pomp and ceremony of a royal garden party, but recreating afternoon tea at home is still very special. During the summer, we have birthday parties in the garden and tea with the whole family. And in wintertime, we cosy up by the fire with family, friends and board games. No TV, no computer, just toast with anchovy butter, chocolate cake (see pages 237 and 124) and a good cuppa — what more could you possibly want?

My hubby's perfect loaf recipe

Paul dictated this recipe to me after we made it together at home. Although it's a bit more complicated than my usual recipe, the result is definitely worth the effort. Freshly baked bread is just the most delicious thing ever, so give it a go.

Makes 1 large loaf

500g stoneground wholemeal flour, plus extra for dusting

40g unsalted butter, softened

10g salt

7g instant yeast

340ml cold water

Put the flour into a large bowl and rub in the butter. Stir in the salt, then the yeast and 250ml of the water. Keep moving the mixture gently around the bowl with your hands until a dough begins to form. Add the remaining water and continue mixing to pick up any remaining flour. Lift the outer edge of the dough and push it with the heel of your hand into the middle. Give the bowl a quarter turn and repeat the lifting and pushing for at least 2 minutes.

Place the dough on a lightly floured work surface, where you are now going to stretch it. Hold the edge nearest you with your fingertips, then use your other hand to pull the dough away from you and roll it back on itself, giving a quarter turn each time. Repeat this process for another 8–10 minutes to build up the gluten. The dough should be soft and smooth. Place in a large, lightly oiled bowl, cover with cling film and leave to rise in a cool room for 2 hours.

Tip the dough on to a lightly floured surface, punch the air out and flatten down. Grab the top and bottom and fold them into the middle. Roll tightly from top to bottom, as if you are making a Swiss roll. You should now have a sausage-shaped dough. Place it seam-side down on a baking sheet lined with baking parchment. Enclose the whole tray inside a plastic carrier bag, tying the handles loosely. Leave to rise for another 1½ hours, until the dough has doubled in size.

Preheat the oven to 200°C/Gas mark 6. At the same time, heat a roasting tray in the bottom of the oven.

Dust the loaf with some flour and, with the flat of your hand, gently rub the flour over the surface of the loaf. Using a sharp knife, make 4 diagonal incisions along your loaf. Place the loaf in the middle of the oven and pour a litre of cold water into the roasting tray at the bottom to create steam. Bake for 25 minutes, then lower the temperature to 190°C/Gas mark 5 and bake for a further 15 minutes. The loaf should be golden brown when done. Place on a wire rack to cool.

Homemade summer berry jam

There is nothing nicer than homemade jam – that's a fact. My mother was a keen pick-your-own jam-maker, and would bundle my sister and me and any other potential small helpers into the car to go to the farm to pick strawberries, raspberries and loganberries for turning into jam for the winter months. This is her simple recipe and it hasn't failed me yet. Use it as a guide for other fruit jams.

Makes about 4 standard jars
900g mixed berries or chopped fruit – blackberries, plums, strawberries, blueberries
900g jam sugar
juice of ½ lemon

Preheat the oven to 150ºC/Gas mark 2. Place a clean saucer in the fridge.

First sterilise 4 jam jars. Wash them well, allow to dry naturally, then place on a baking tray in the oven for about 30 minutes.

Meanwhile, place the fruit in a large stainless steel pan with the sugar and lemon juice. Crush a little with a potato masher, then stir over a low heat until the sugar dissolves. Turn up the heat until you have a rolling boil, stirring often. When the jam thickens, remove the saucer from the fridge and drop a little of the mixture into the middle. Allow to cool for a minute or so: if it forms a slight skin that wrinkles when pushed with a finger, it's ready; if not, carry on boiling until it does. When ready, remove the pan from the heat, stir and allow to cool for about 15 minutes.

Using oven gloves, remove the jars from the oven. Spoon the jam into the jars, leaving about a 2cm gap at the top. I usually cut circles of greaseproof paper to sit on top of the jam, then cover the neck of the jars with cellophane, secure it with an elastic band and replace the lid. (Some people just use greaseproof and a lid, or cellophane on its own – the choice is yours.) Store in a dry cool place.

Anchovy butter

Possibly the most scrumptious thing to spread on hot buttered toast on a cold, windy day, this can also be melted over grilled lamb chops – delish!

175g slightly salted butter, at room temperature

6–8 anchovy fillets

freshly ground black pepper

Cut some greaseproof paper into a rectangle a little larger than a 450g butter wrapper.

Put the anchovies into a bowl and mash with a fork. Add the butter a bit at a time with a good twist of pepper, mashing well after each addition.

Scrape the mixture into the centre of the greaseproof paper. Fold one edge over it and start rolling the butter into a cylinder shape within the paper. When you have done this, tightly twist both ends of the paper (like a toffee) and chill in the fridge.

To serve, slice into rounds and eat with toast.

35g smoked salmon, finely chopped

150g unsalted butter

7g dill, chopped

salt and freshly ground black pepper

Smoked salmon and dill butter

My great grandma was Norwegian and therefore a huge salmon fan. This is a take on her recipe, and is perfect with slices of brown wholemeal bread (see page 233). You can also use it melted on pasta for a quick supper, or stuffed into baked potatoes and sprinkled with black pepper.

Cut some greaseproof paper into a rectangle a little larger than a 450g butter wrapper.

Put the salmon into a bowl, then mix in the butter, dill and seasoning.

Scrape the mixture into the centre of the greaseproof paper. Fold one edge over it and start rolling the butter into a cylinder shape within the paper. When you have done this, tightly twist both ends of the paper (like a toffee) and chill in the fridge.

To serve, slice into rounds and eat with toast.

Oven shorties

These biscuits are best eaten straight from the oven while they are still warm, and are also lovely served with poached fruit or the Syllabub (see page 186 or 214). The basic dough recipe is really useful because you can add whatever flavour you like – a few drops of rose water, almond extract, lemon zest, or even chocolate chips and chopped nuts.

Makes about 20

200g salted butter, at room temperature

100g caster sugar, plus a little extra for sprinkling

200g plain flour

100g semolina

1 tsp cornflour

Put the butter and sugar in a bowl and beat together until pale and creamy. Sift in the flour, semolina and cornflour, then use your hands to form the mixture into a dough. Knead lightly to fully combine, then roll into a sausage shape about 3–4cm in diameter. Wrap in greaseproof paper or cling film and store in the fridge until you're ready to bake.

Preheat the oven to 180°C/Gas mark 4. Line a baking sheet with baking parchment.

Cut the dough into circles 1cm thick and place them about 2cm apart on the prepared sheet. Bake for 15–20 minutes, until pale golden brown. Sprinkle with a little caster sugar and cool on a wire rack.

Strawberry and white chocolate rocky road

What can I say about this? White chocolate, pistachios and strawberries ... heaven! Children always love rocky road, and you really can use up whatever odds and ends you have in your cupboard — broken biscuits, mini marshmallows, dried fruits, oddments of chocolate, Turkish delight — just mix it all in. I sometimes top it all with a layer of melted dark chocolate scattered with freeze-dried strawberries or raspberries — so pretty — perfect for a birthday or any time, really. Cut it into pieces and pile it high. Nom-nom-nom!

Makes about 20 squares

butter, for greasing

600g good-quality white chocolate

150g shelled pistachios, crushed

150g dried cranberries, chopped

1 x 7g tube freeze-dried strawberries, halved

100g pink and white mini marshmallows

handful of rose petals

Grease a medium baking dish and line it with greaseproof paper.

Melt the chocolate in a heatproof bowl set over a saucepan of simmering water (make sure the bowl doesn't actually touch the water).

Combine the pistachios, cranberries, strawberries and marshmallows in a bowl. Pour the melted chocolate over them and stir gently to combine. Tip the mixture into the prepared dish and pat down firmly. Place in the fridge to set for at least 2 hours.

Cut the set mixture into squares with a sharp knife. Serve on a dish, scattered with the rose petals.

Grandma's fruitcake

For as long as I can remember, my mother has made this cake once a week so that there is always a slice for elevenses, something to offer an unexpected visitor, and a treat for Sunday afternoon tea with all the family. It is rich and fruity with lovely, buttery crumbs. It's the cake I most like to have, sitting with Mum in her pretty garden with a cup of tea. Happy days.

Serves 6–8

butter, for greasing

300g sultanas

250ml orange juice

1 tbsp brandy

1 tbsp honey

140g soft margarine

80g caster sugar

50g demerara sugar

2 large eggs

225g self-raising flour

1 tsp ground ginger

½ tsp ground mixed spice

5 tbsp milk

zest of 1 orange

Preheat the oven to 150°C/Gas mark 2. Butter an 18cm loose-bottomed cake tin and line it with baking parchment.

Put the sultanas in a large bowl with the orange juice, brandy and honey and set aside to soak for as long as you can.

Put the margarine and both sugars into another bowl and whisk until pale and creamy. Beat in the eggs one at a time with a spoonful of the flour. Using a spoon, mix in the remaining flour, spices and milk along with the orange zest.

Drain the sultanas and fold them into the cake batter. Pour into the prepared tin and bake for about 2 hours. The time depends on your oven, so make sure you don't overcook the cake – it is ready when a skewer inserted in the centre comes out clean. Put the kettle on and cut a slice!

My lovely mummy Gloria Moores in her garden with her beloved roses, with me and my sister. Her fruitcake recipe for afternoon tea always makes me think of her in her garden in the summertime.

Raspberry chocolate bombes

Chocolatey and gooey with a blast of fresh raspberry in the middle, and finger-licking sticky icing on the outside, these little cakes are always a favourite with the younger members of the family – and the oldest!

Makes 10–12

125g good-quality dark chocolate

175g unsalted buter

3 eggs, separated

175g caster sugar

55g plain flour

30g ground almonds

pinch of salt

12 frozen raspberries

1 x 10g tube freeze-dried raspberry pieces

For the icing

200ml double cream

200g Bourneville chocolate (36% cocoa solids)

Preheat the oven to 190°C/Gas mark 5. Line a 12-hole bun tin with paper cases.

Put the chocolate and butter in a heatproof bowl set over a saucepan of simmering water (the bowl must not actually touch the water). Heat, stirring now and again, until melted, then set aside.

Put the eggs yolks and sugar into a bowl and beat together. Slowly add the cooling chocolate mixture, stirring as you do so. Sift in the flour and stir to combine. Add the ground almonds and salt and stir again.

Put the egg whites into a clean bowl and whisk into stiff peaks. Gently fold them into the chocolate mixture.

Half-fill each paper case with the mixture, pop a frozen raspberry on top, then cover with the remaining chocolate mixture. Place in the middle of the oven and bake for 20–25 minutes, until risen. Set aside to cool in the tin.

To make the icing, gently heat the cream until hot without allowing it to boil. Lower the heat, then break in the chocolate and stir until melted. Set aside to cool slightly.

Remove the cakes from their paper cases and place on a wire rack. Once cool, spoon some icing over each one and sprinkle with the freeze-dried raspberries. Allow a couple of hours to set, then pop into fresh paper cases and serve.

INDEX

First published in Great Britain in 2015 by Hodder & Stoughton
An Hachette UK company

1

Copyright © Alex Hollywood 2015

Photography Copyright © Dan Jones 2015

The right of Alex Hollywood to be identified as the Author of the Work has been asserted
by her in accordance with the Copyright, Designs and Patents Act 1988.

All rights reserved. No part of this publication may be reproduced, stored in a retrieval
system, or transmitted, in any form or by any means without the prior written
permission of the publisher, nor be otherwise circulated in any form of binding or cover
other than that in which it is published and without a similar condition being imposed on
the subsequent purchaser.

A CIP catalogue record for this title is available from the British Library

Hardback ISBN 978 1 444 79920 0
Ebook ISBN 978 1 444 9922 4

Editorial Director NICKY ROSS
Project Editor SARAH HAMMOND
Copy Editor TRISH BURGESS
Design & Art Direction MIRANDA HARVEY
Photographer DAN JONES
Food Stylist EMMA MILLER

Typeset in Antwerp and Wood Bonnet Antique

Printed and bound in Germany by Mohn media

Hodder & Stoughton policy is to use papers that are natural, renewable and recyclable
products and made from wood grown in sustainable forests. The logging and
manufacturing processes are expected to conform to the environmental regulations of
the country of origin.

Hodder & Stoughton Ltd
338 Euston Road
London NW1 3BH

www.hodder.co.uk

ACKNOWLEDGEMENTS

I would firstly like to thank Borra, my agent, for helping me set out on this journey as well as lovely Nicky Ross from Hodder & Stoughton for giving me the opportunity to write this, my very first book. A huge thanks to photographer Dan Jones for his patience with dealing with me and Rufus, my exuberant Labrador, and also thanks to the rest of the Hodder team for their tireless efforts getting the book just right.

To my wonderful home economist and friend Kirsty, a huge thank you for being on call 24/7, and to the rest of my fab friends, I couldn't have done it without you! To my husband Paul and son Josh, thank you for your patience, your love and your support.

Finally my love and thanks to my sister – my friend and my rock – and to my mother, Gloria, Grandmother Vanda and Great Grandmother Kari, all that I am, I owe to you…